Answer Key

UNDERSTANDING AND USING

ENGLISH GRAMMAR

Third Edition

Betty Schrampfer Azar

PRENTICE HALL REGENTS

Upper Saddle River, NJ 07458

Publisher: *Mary Jane Peluso*
Development Editor: *Janet Johnston*
AVP/Director of Production and Manufacturing: *Aliza Greenblatt*
Executive Managing Editor: *Dominick Mosco*
Managing Editor: *Shelley Hartle*
Electronic Production Editor: *Noël Vreeland Carter*
Cover Designer: *Eric Dawson*
Manufacturing Manager: *Ray Keating*

© 1999 by Betty Schrampfer Azar
Published by Prentice Hall Regents
Prentice-Hall, Inc.
Upper Saddle River, New Jersey 07458

Printed in the United States of America

10 9 8 7 6 5 4

ISBN 0-13-020552-4

Prentice-Hall International (UK) Limited,London
Prentice-Hall of Australia Pty. Limited, Sydney
Prentice-Hall Canada Inc., Toronto
Prentice-Hall Hispanoamericana, S.A., Mexico
Prentice-Hall of India Private Limited, New Delhi
Prentice-Hall of Japan, Inc., Tokyo
Pearson Education Asia Pte. Ltd., Singapore
Editora Prentice-Hall do Brasil, Ltda., Rio de Janeiro

Table of Contents

		Page
Chapter 1	OVERVIEW OF VERB TENSES	1
Chapter 2	PRESENT AND PAST, SIMPLE AND PROGRESSIVE	4
Chapter 3	PERFECT AND PERFECT PROGRESSIVE TENSES	8
Chapter 4	FUTURE TIME	11
Chapter 5	ADVERB CLAUSES OF TIME AND REVIEW OF VERB TENSES	14
Chapter 6	SUBJECT-VERB AGREEMENT	18
Chapter 7	NOUNS	21
Chapter 8	PRONOUNS	26
Chapter 9	MODALS, PART 1	30
Chapter 10	MODALS, PART 2	32
Chapter 11	THE PASSIVE	35
Chapter 12	NOUN CLAUSES	41
Chapter 13	ADJECTIVE CLAUSES	48
Chapter 14	GERUNDS AND INFINITIVES, PART 1	59
Chapter 15	GERUNDS AND INFINITIVES, PART 2	67
Chapter 16	COORDINATING CONJUNCTIONS	71
Chapter 17	ADVERB CLAUSES	76
Chapter 18	REDUCTION OF ADVERB CLAUSES TO MODIFYING ADVERBIAL PHRASES	80
Chapter 19	CONNECTIVES THAT EXPRESS CAUSE AND EFFECT, CONTRAST, AND CONDITION	85
Chapter 20	CONDITIONAL SENTENCES AND WISHES	97
Appendix	SUPPLEMENTARY GRAMMAR UNITS	102

Errata

NOTE: The answers given in this *Answer Key* reflect corrections made in the textbook after the first printing. These corrections are listed below.

If you find further errors in the text, please e-mail Prentice Hall Regents at phr_web@prenhall.com (with "for Betty" in the subject box).

CHAPTER 1, Exercise 3, p. 3: The last question in Item 3 should be renumbered item 4:
4. What are you going to do tomorrow?

CHAPTER 2, Exercise 12, p. 21: The last chart heading should read: /əd/ NOT /əz/.

CHAPTER 5, Exercise 15, p. 80: Number (7) should begin with the sentence currently numbered (8). All numbers thereafter should be changed. The total numbert of answers in the exercise should be (22) NOT (23).

CHAPTER 6, Exercise 2, p. 85: The second column in Group C contains two items numbered 30. Instead of 30 through 34 the second column should be numbered 30 through 35.

CHAPTER 11, Exercise 6, p. 213: Item 4 should read: "Someone has given Maria a promotion at her job as a computer programmer at Microsoft."

CHAPTER 13, Exercise 2, p. 269: Item 5 should read: "The man is standing over there. Ann brought him to the party."

CHAPTER 13, Exercise 23, p. 282: Remove the commas in Item 8.

CHAPTER 15, Exercise 2, p. 327: In Item 4, the preposition "for" should be "to" before the write-on rule.

CHAPTER 17, Exercise 8, p. 366: Item 6 should read: "Jack is an interesting storyteller and conversationalist, whereas his brother _____ ."

CHAPTER 17, Exercise 12, p. 369: Item 10 should read: "I'm going to . . . whether . . . or not."

<u>CHAPTER 18, Exercise 6, p. 378</u>: Item 9 in Column A should read: "She has done very well in her studies."

<u>CHAPTER 19, Exercise 28, p. 402</u>: The title of this exercise should read: "Expressing conditions. (Chart 19-8)."

<u>CHAPTER 20, Exercise 7, p. 418</u>: There are two items numbered "10." The second one (at the top of page 419) should be number "11."

<u>CHAPTER 20, Exercise 25, p. 430</u>: The item at the top of page 431 should be "4," NOT "2."

<u>CHAPTER 20, Exercise 30, p. 435</u>: The parentheses in Speaker B's line should read: "*(have)*" NOT "*(have, not).*"

<u>APPENDIX, Exercise 21, p. A21</u>: The chart of preposition combinations should read (under the "E" column): "excel in, at"

<u>APPENDIX, Exercise 15, p. A16</u>: Item 15 should read: "There is something wrong with Jane today, _____ ?"

<u>APPENDIX, Exercise 11, p. A11</u>: Item 18 should read: "Because the traffic was heavy. I was late because the traffic was heavy."

CHAPTER 18, Exercise 6, p. 378: Item 9 in Column A should read: "She has done very well in her studies."

CHAPTER 19, Exercise 28, p. 402: The title of this exercise should read: "Expressing conditions. (Chart 19-8)."

CHAPTER 20, Exercise 7, p. 418: There are two items numbered "10." The second one (at the top of page 419) should be number "11."

CHAPTER 20, Exercise 25, p. 430: The item at the top of page 431 should be "4," NOT "2."

CHAPTER 20, Exercise 30, p. 435: The parentheses in Speaker B's line should read: "(have)" NOT "(have, not)."

APPENDIX, Exercise 21, p. A21: The chart of preposition combinations should read (under the "E" column): "excel in, at"

Chapter One: OVERVIEW OF VERB TENSES

EXERCISE 1, p. 1. *Introductions and interviews.*

Questions only. **1.** What is your name? **2.** How do you spell your (last) name? / How do you spell that? **3.** Where are you from? / What country are you from? / What is your hometown? / Where were you born? **4.** Where are you living? / Where do you live? **5.** How long have you been living (in this place/here)? How long do you plan to be / are you planning to be / are you going to be (in this place/here)? **6.** Why did you (decide to) come here? **7.** [If a student]: What is your major / your field of study? / What are you studying? [If an employee]: What kind of work do you do? / What do you do? **8.** What do you like to do in your spare time? / Do you have any hobbies? **9.** How are you getting along? **10.** How do you like living here? / What do you think of (this place)?

EXERCISE 2, p. 2. *Overview of verb tenses.*

Questions only. **1.** What do you do every day before you leave home? **2.** What did you do last night? **3.** What were you doing at (this exact time) yesterday? **4.** What are you doing right now? **5.** What have you done since you got up this morning? **6.** What have you been doing for the past five minutes? **7.** What will you do/are you going to do tomorrow? **8.** What will you be doing at (this exact time) tomorrow? **9.** What had you done by the time you got here today? **10.** What will you have done by the time you go to bed tonight?

EXERCISE 3, p. 3. *The simple tenses.*

Possible responses: **1.** The sun rises in the east. Water and oil don't mix. **2.** Every day I get out of bed, get dressed, and have breakfast. **3.** Yesterday I took the bus to school, went to class, and cooked dinner. **4.** Tomorrow is Saturday, so I am going to do my laundry.

EXERCISE 4, p. 3. *The progressive tenses.*

Possible responses: **1.** Right now I am doing Exercise 4. My classmates are looking at their grammar books. It is raining outside the classroom. **2.** At two o'clock this morning, I was at home. I was sleeping. **3.** At two o'clock tomorrow morning I will be at home. I will be sleeping.

EXERCISE 5, p. 4. *The perfect tenses.*

Possible responses: **1.** Yes, I have already eaten today. I had lunch at noon.
2. Yes, I had eaten three meals before I went to bed last night. **3.** Yes, by the time I go to bed tonight, I will have had dinner.

EXERCISE 6, p. 5. *The perfect progressive tenses.*

Possible responses: **1.** Right now I am doing an exercise in my grammar book. I have been doing the exercise for ten minutes. **2.** Last night at nine o'clock I was doing my English homework. I stopped doing my homework at ten o'clock. I stopped doing my homework because my eyes were tired. I had been doing my English homework for two hours before I stopped. **3.** At nine o'clock tomorrow night, I am going to be doing my English homework. I am going to stop doing my English homework at ten o'clock. I need to go to sleep at ten o'clock. I will have been doing my English homework for one hour before I stop.

EXERCISE 7, p. 8. *Overview of verb tenses.*

2. The speakers are discussing an activity that began and ended in the past. Tense: the simple past **3.** The speakers are discussing an activity that is happening (is in progress) at the moment of speaking. Tense: the present progressive **4.** The speakers are discussing an activity in progress at a particular time in the past. Tense: the past progressive **5.** The speakers are discussing activities that have occurred (or not occurred) "before now," at unspecific times in the past. Tense: the present perfect **6.** The speakers are discussing what will happen at a specific time in the future. Tense: the simple future **7.** This question concerns an activity that will be in progress at a particular time in the future. Tense: the future progressive **8.** This question concerns the duration of an activity that started in the past and is still in progress. Tense: the present perfect progressive **9.** The speakers are talking about the duration of an activity that has already started and will end at a specific time in the future. Tense: the future perfect progressive **10.** This question concerns an activity that started and ended before another time in the past. Tense: the past perfect **11.** This question concerns an activity that will be finished before a particular time in the future. Tense: the future perfect **12.** This question concerns the duration of an activity that began before another time in the past. Tense: the past perfect progressive

EXERCISE 8, p. 9. *Overview of verb tenses.*

Possible responses: **1.** I brush my teeth every day. **2.** I combed my hair yesterday. **3.** Tomorrow I will hug my children and kiss my wife/husband.
4. Right now I am talking to you. [*Note: The* Answer Key *gives the full, uncontracted*

forms of verbs rather than contracting them with pronoun subjects. Auxiliary verbs such as "will" and "am" are usually contracted in speech. See Appendix Unit C.]   **5.** At this time yesterday, I was watching a game on TV.   **6.** At this time tomorrow I will be sitting right here.   **7.** Since I got up this morning, I have eaten breakfast and have come to school.   **8.** Before I went to bed last night, I had eaten dinner, done my homework, and read the newspaper.   **9.** By the time I go to bed tonight, I will have watched the news on TV.   **10.** I am talking to you. I have been talking to you for ten minutes.   **11.** Before Ms. Foley walked into the classroom today, I was chatting with the student next to me. I had been doing that for five minutes.   **12.** Tomorrow before Ms. Foley walks into the classroom, I will be talking to the student who sits next to me. I will have been talking to him/her for four or five minutes before Ms. Foley walks into the classroom.

EXERCISE 9, p. 9. *Error analysis: questions and negative verb forms.*
   1. Does Pedro <u>walk</u> to work every morning?   **2.** What <u>are you</u> talking about? I <u>don't</u> understand you.   **3.** Did you <u>finish</u> your work?   **4.** My friend doesn't <u>like</u> her apartment.   **5.** Do you <u>work</u> for this company?   OR   <u>Are you</u> working for this company?   **6.** What time <u>did</u> your plane arrive?   **7.** How long have you <u>been</u> living in this city?   OR   How long have you <u>lived</u> in this city?   **8.** My brother <u>doesn't</u> have <u>a</u> job right now.   **9.** Ali <u>won't</u> ~~to~~ be in class tomorrow.
   10. I <u>hadn't seen</u> snow before I moved to Canada last year.   OR   I <u>had</u> never <u>seen</u> snow before I moved to Canada last year.

EXERCISE 10, p. 10. *Spelling pretest.*
   1. hoped   **2.** dining   **3.** stopped   **4.** planning   **5.** rained
   6. waiting   **7.** listening   **8.** happened   **9.** beginning   **10.** occurred
   11. starting   **12.** warned   **13.** enjoyed   **14.** playing   **15.** studying
   16. worried   **17.** died   **18.** lying

EXERCISE 11, p. 11. *Spelling of* -ING *and* -ED *forms.*
   PART I.   **2.** hiding   **3.** running   **4.** ruining   **5.** coming   **6.** writing
   7. eating   **8.** sitting   **9.** acting   **10.** patting   **11.** opening
   12. beginning   **13.** earning   **14.** frying   **15.** dying   **16.** employing

   PART II.   **2.** trying, tried   **3.** staying, stayed   **4.** taping, taped
   5. tapping, tapped   **6.** offering, offered   **7.** preferring, preferred
   8. gaining, gained   **9.** planning, planned   **10.** tying, tied   **11.** helping, helped
   12. studying, studied   **13.** admitting, admitted   **14.** visiting, visited
   15. hugging, hugged   **16.** raging, raged

EXERCISE 12, p. 11. *Spelling of -ING and -ED forms.*

PART I.   2. jarred   3. jeered   4. dotted   5. looted   6. pointed
7. exited   8. permitted   9. intensified   10. destroyed   11. suffered
12. occurred

PART II.   14. riding   15. bidding   16. burying   17. decaying
18. tying   19. taming   20. teeming   21. trimming   22. harming
23. ripening   24. regretting

~~~~~~~~~~~~~~~~~

~~~~~~~~~~~~~~~~~

Chapter Two: PRESENT AND PAST, SIMPLE AND PROGRESSIVE

EXERCISE 1, p. 12. *Preview: present and past verbs.*

2. I <u>don't know</u> Sam's wife.   3. A: What <u>are you</u> talking about?   B: I <u>am</u> talking about the political situation in my country.   4. My roommate usually <u>watches</u> TV, <u>listens</u> to music, or <u>goes</u> out in the evening.   5. When I turned on the ignition key, the car <u>started</u>.   6. This class <u>consists</u> of students who <u>want</u> to learn English.
7. The children <u>drew</u> some pictures in school this morning.   8. While Tom <u>was</u> reading in bed last night, his phone <u>rang</u>. When he <u>answered</u> it, the caller <u>hung</u> up.
9. Right now Sally <u>is</u> in the kitchen eating breakfast.   10. When the sun <u>rises</u>, it <u>appears</u> from below the horizon.

EXERCISE 4, p. 14. *Simple present vs. present progressive.*

2. washes   3. usually sits . . . is sitting   4. am trying   5. Do you always lock   6. am still waiting   7. is shining   8. shines . . . wakes
9. A: is snowing   B: doesn't snow   10. A: am I doing   B: are rubbing . . . are rubbing

EXERCISE 6, p. 16. *Verbs that have both stative and progressive meanings.*

1. a. *smell* describes a state that exists, i.e., the flowers have a smell and that smell is good.
   b. *is smelling* describes the action of using one's nose.
2. a. *think* means "believe" in this sentence and describes a state.
   b. *am thinking* is an action; thoughts are going through the speaker's mind.
3. a. *see* describes a perception that exists right now as a result of the speaker using his/her eyes.
   b. *is seeing a doctor* means "is going to a doctor for help," a general activity in progress at present.
   c. *are seeing* means they are dating each other, a general activity in progress at present.
4. a. *looks* means "appears or seems to be" and describes an apparent state that exists: Kathy is apparently cold.
   b. *is looking* describes the action of using one's eyes.
5. a. *appears* means "seems" and describes an apparent state that exists.
   b. *is appearing* describes the action of performing on stage in a theater, a general activity in progress at present.
6. a. *is feeling* describes the action of using one's sense of touch. Sue is using her hands to touch the cat's fur. The activity is in progress at the present moment.
   b. *feels* describes a state that exists, the state of the cat's fur; i.e., it is soft.
   c. *am not feeling* describes the speaker's physical feelings of illness, in progress at the present. [*Note: The simple present is also possible here with little difference in meaning* (I don't feel well today) *to describe a state that exists.*]
   d. *feel* means "think or believe" in this sentence and describes a state.
7. a. *has* means "owns" here and describes a state that exists.
   b. *am having* and *is having* mean "experiencing" and describe activities in progress.
8. a. *remember* describes a state that exists.
   b. *is remembering* describes an activity in progress: memories are going through Aunt Sara's mind.
9. a. *weighs* describes a state that exists.
   b. *is weighing* describes an activity in progress: the grocer is putting the bananas on a scale and reading what the scale says.

EXERCISE 7, p. 17. AM / IS / ARE BEING + *adjective.*

2. careful, kind, responsible   3. polite, quiet   4. cruel, unfair, unpleasant
5. good, noisy

EXERCISE 8, p. 18. *Simple present vs. present progressive.*

2. is beginning . . . don't have . . . is wearing   **3.** don't own . . . wear   **4.** sleep . . . get . . . study   **5.** is taking . . . don't want . . . needs   **6.** am looking . . . looks . . . has . . . isn't having   **7.** am looking . . . is writing . . . is biting . . . is scratching . . . is staring . . . seems . . . is thinking . . . do you think . . . is doing   **8.** want . . . know . . . means . . . does "sword" mean   **9.** is doing . . . is being . . . doesn't want . . . is always

EXERCISE 10, p. 20. *Pronunciation of -ED endings.*

2. sob/d/   **3.** grade/əd/   **4.** ask/t/   **5.** help/t/   **6.** watch/t/
7. fill/d/   **8.** defend/əd/   **9.** pour/d/   **10.** wait/əd/   **11.** enjoy/d/
12. load/əd/   **13.** roam/d/   **14.** kiss/t/   **15.** halt/əd/
16. laugh/t/   **17.** dry/d/   **18.** believe/d/   **19.** judge/d/
20. count/əd/   **21.** add/əd/   **22.** box/t/   **23.** rest/əd/
24. push/t/

EXERCISE 11, p. 21. *Pronunciation of -ED endings.*

2. hope/t   **3.** mop/t/ . . . vacuum/d/ . . . dust/əd/   **4.** last/əd/   **5.** tap/t
6. describe/d/   **7.** demand/əd/   **8.** push/t/ . . . pull/d/   **9.** hand/əd/
10. toot/əd/   **11.** ask/t/   **12.** flood/əd/   **13.** depart/əd/ . . . land/əd/
14. jump/t/ . . . shout/əd/

EXERCISE 13, p. 24. *Oral review of irregular verbs.*

Partial responses: **1.** Yes, I drank . . . .   **2.** brought   **3.** forgot   **4.** shook
5. caught   **6.** drove   **7.** lost   **8.** mislaid   **9.** found   **10.** understood
11. told   **12.** spread   **13.** fell   **14.** hurt   **15.** flew   **16.** wore
17. hung   **18.** ate   **19.** took   **20.** rode   **21.** swore   **22.** forgave
23. wrote   **24.** No! I didn't bite the dog. The dog bit me.

EXERCISE 14, p. 24. *Oral review of irregular verbs.*

Partial responses: **1.** No, someone else made . . . .   **2.** broke   **3.** stole
4. took   **5.** drew   **6.** swept   **7.** taught   **8.** dug   **9.** fed   **10.** hid
11. blew   **12.** threw   **13.** tore   **14.** built   **15.** spoke   **16.** wove

EXERCISE 15, p. 25. *Oral review of irregular verbs.*

Partial responses: **1.** Yes, I gave . . . .   **2.** stood   **3.** chose   **4.** ran
5. slept   **6.** heard   **7.** withdrew   **8.** woke up   **9.** swam   **10.** went
11. bent   **12.** sent   **13.** sang   **14.** stuck   **15.** ground   **16.** struck
17. lit   **18.** meant   **19.** held   **20.** spoke

EXERCISE 16, p. 25. *Oral review of irregular verbs.*

Partial responses: **1.** Yes, it began . . . . **2.** rose **3.** cut **4.** bled
5. grew **6.** stung **7.** rang **8.** froze **9.** quit **10.** fought
11. crept **12.** shot **13.** fled **14.** won **15.** slid **16.** swung
17. blew **18.** burst **19.** broadcast **20.** knew

EXERCISE 17, p. 26. *Troublesome verbs.*

1. raised **2.** rises **3.** sat **4.** set **5.** lay **6.** lying **7.** laid
8. lie **9.** lies **10.** raises **11.** rose **12.** lays **13.** laid
14. set **15.** sat **16.** lies

EXERCISE 19, p. 28. *Simple past vs. past progressive.*

2. didn't want . . . was raining **3.** called . . . wasn't . . . was studying **4.** didn't
hear . . . was sleeping **5.** was shining . . . was blowing . . . were singing
6. were arguing . . . walked **7.** opened . . . found **8.** was reading . . . fell . . .
closed . . . tiptoed **9.** was waiting **10.** A: Did you hear B: wasn't listening
. . . was thinking **11.** A: did you break B: slipped . . . was crossing **12.** was
she wearing **13.** finally found . . . was already . . . were talking busily . . . were
speaking . . . were conversing . . . were just sitting . . . chose . . . sat . . . walked . . .
stopped **14.** was snowing . . . was shining . . . were shoveling . . . was lying

EXERCISE 23, p. 31. *Using progressive verbs with* ALWAYS.

2. e. He's always leaving his dirty dishes on the table. **3.** c. He's forever
borrowing my clothes without asking me. **4.** a. He's constantly bragging about
himself. **5.** f. He's always trying to show me he's smarter than me.
6. g. He's constantly cracking his knuckles while I'm trying to study. **7.** d.
He's always forgetting to give me my phone messages. **8.** *(free response)*

EXERCISE 24, p. 32. *Using expressions of place with progressive verbs.*

PART I. **3.** He was in his bedroom watching TV. **4.** He was watching TV in his
bedroom. **5.** He is taking a nap on the couch in the living room. **6.** He is on the
couch in the living room taking a nap. **7.** She is in Singapore attending a
conference.

PART II. (Possible completions.) **9.** He's upstairs getting his books. **10.** She's
in her office correcting test papers. **11.** She's in the kitchen washing dishes.
12. He was at home resting from his long trip. **13.** He was in New York
attending a basketball game.

PART III. (*Possible completions.*) **15.** I'm back to work now, but a month ago I was <u>on the beach</u> lying in the sun. **16.** We are <u>in class</u> studying English grammar. **17.** No one could see the thief because he was <u>in the garbage can</u> hiding from the police. **18.** When I saw Diana, she was <u>in the Registrar's Office</u> trying to find out what she was supposed to do.

EXERCISE 25, p. 33. *Error analysis: present and past verbs.*

1. I always <u>eat</u> breakfast. **2.** <u>While</u> I was working in my office yesterday, my cousin <u>stopped</u> by to visit me. **3.** Portual <u>lies</u> to the west of Spain. **4.** Yuki <u>stayed</u> home because she <u>caught</u> / <u>was catching</u> / <u>had caught</u> a bad cold. **5.** My brother <u>looks</u> like our father, but I <u>resemble</u> my mother. **6.** As a verb, "sink" <u>means</u> "move downward." What <u>does</u> it <u>mean</u> as a noun? **7.** Sang-Joon, are you <u>listening</u> to me? I am <u>talking</u> to you! **8.** I <u>rewound</u> the rented video before I <u>returned</u> it to the store yesterday. **9.** Abdallah <u>wants</u> a snack. He's ~~being~~ <u>hungry</u>. **10.** Anna <u>raised</u> her eyebrows in surprise. **11.** Yesterday I was working at my computer when Shelley <u>came</u> to the door of my office. I <u>didn't know</u> she was there. I was <u>concentrating</u> hard on my work. When she suddenly <u>spoke</u>, I <u>jumped</u>. She <u>startled</u> me. **12.** While I was surfing the net yesterday, I <u>found</u> a really interesting website. [*also possible:* Web site]

~~~~~~~~~~~~~~~~~
~~~~~~~~~~~~~~~~~

Chapter Three: PERFECT AND PERFECT PROGRESSIVE TENSES

EXERCISE 1, p. 34. *Review of irregular past participles.*

Questions only: Have you ever . . . ?

1. bought	**2.** broken	**3.** hidden	**4.** taught	**5.** made	**6.** won
7. flown	**8.** spoken	**9.** stolen	**10.** fallen	**11.** held	**12.** fed
13. built	**14.** forgotten	**15.** understood		**16.** eaten	

EXERCISE 2, p. 35. *Review: regular and irregular past participles.*

Questions only: Have you ever . . . ?

1. climbed	**2.** written	**3.** been	**4.** told	**5.** smoked	**6.** ridden
7. taught	**8.** seen	**9.** met	**10.** given	**11.** eaten	**12.** studied
13. played	**14.** gone	**15.** walked	**16.** watched	**17.** taken	**18.** driven
19. fallen	**20.** had	**21.** driven	**22.** read	**23.** drawn	**24.** ridden
25. caught	**26.** slept	**27.** written	**28.** lost	**29.** had	**30.** brought
31. worn	**32.** drunk	**33.** left	**34.** dug	**35.** shaken	**36.** sung

EXERCISE 3, p. 36. *Present perfect vs. simple past.*

2. went   **3.** arrived   **4.** has been   **5.** have already missed . . . missed
6. have had   **7.** has drawn . . . drew   **8.** has called . . . called   **9.** has worn . . .
wore   **10.** has risen . . . rose   **11.** saw   **12.** has never seen [*"never saw"*
would mean that either Fatima is now dead or you are telling a story about a fictional
character who lived in the past.]   **13.** have known [*"knew" would mean that Greg*
Adams is, in all likelihood, dead.]   **14.** has just arrived / just arrived
15. haven't been . . . hasn't responded . . . started . . . have faxed . . . have phoned . . .
have sent

EXERCISE 4, p. 37. *Present perfect.*

Possible responses: **1.** I've bought six books . . . .   OR   I haven't bought any . . . .
2. I've gotten two . . . .   OR   I haven't gotten any . . . .   **3.** I've written three . . . .
OR   I haven't written any . . . .   **4.** You've asked three questions . . . .
5. I've flown many times . . . .   **6.** I have made dinner many times . . . .
7. I've met lots of people . . . .   **8.** I haven't missed any classes . . . .
9. I've had two cups . . . .   **10.** I've had four classes . . . .   **11.** I've eaten
at a restaurant several times . . . .   **12.** I've ridden a bike lots of times.

EXERCISE 5, p. 38. *Present perfect.*

Possible responses: **2.** two weeks . . . two weeks . . . the twenty-second of
September   **3.** October 2 . . . September 2 OR one month ago . . . September 2 . . .
one month   **4.** 1999 . . . 1981 . . . eighteen years . . . 1981   **5.** In October . . .
three months . . . October

EXERCISE 7, p. 39. *Present perfect.*

3. "weather's" been   **4.** "neighbors've" asked   **5.** "teacher's" never eaten
6. *(no contraction; "has" is the main verb)*   **7.** "parents've" lived   **8.** *(no*
contraction; "have" is the main verb)   **9.** "Where've" you been?
10. "What've" you done

EXERCISE 8, p. 40. *Present perfect vs. simple past.*
   1. came . . . have you made   2. haven't had . . . have had   3. had . . . went
   4. have gotten/got [*"got" is principally British usage*] . . . saw . . . have also
   gotten/got   5. advanced   6. have made   7. have changed . . . were . . . have
   become . . . has also changed . . . were   8. have already taken . . . took
   9. A: Have you   B: haven't   10. have never eaten   11. Have you eaten . . .
   have already eaten . . . have just finished   OR   Did you eat . . . already ate . . . just
   finished   12. A: have you visited   B: have been   A: have never been . . .
   were you   B: also visited . . . took   A: did you visit . . .   A: have always
   wanted . . . haven't had . . . went . . . haven't gone

EXERCISE 10, p. 42. *Error analysis: present perfect progressive.*
   1. They <u>have been</u> playing for almost two hours.   2. He <u>has been talking</u> on the
   phone for more than half an hour.   3. I <u>have been trying</u> to study for the last hour,
   but something always seems to interrupt me.   4. He <u>has been</u> waiting there for the
   last twenty minutes.

EXERCISE 11, p. 43. *Present perfect vs. present perfect progressive.*
   1. has been snowing   2. have had   3. have been studying   4. have
   written   5. has rung   6. has been ringing   7. Have you been . . . have
   been trying   8. haven't seen . . . have you been doing   9. have never had
   10. Have you been crying?   11· A: has he been   B: has been teaching/has
   taught   12. has been playing

EXERCISE 15, p. 46. *Simple past vs. past perfect.*
   1. was . . . became   2. felt . . . took   3. had already given . . . got
   4. was . . . had stopped   5. roamed . . . had become . . . appeared   6. had
   never seen . . . visited   7. saw . . . hadn't seen . . . didn't recognize . . . had lost
   8. emigrated . . . had never traveled . . . settled . . . grew . . . went . . . had always
   wanted

EXERCISE 17, p. 48. *Present perfect progressive and past perfect progressive.*
   3. have been studying   4. had been studying   5. had been daydreaming
   6. have been sleeping

EXERCISE 18, p. 48. *Review of verb tenses.*
   2. Gloria   3. Ken   4. Mr. Sanchez   5. Alice   6. Joe
   7. Carlos   8. Jane   9. Mr. Fox

10

EXERCISE 19, p. 49. *Error analysis: present and past verbs.*

1. Since I came to this country, I <u>have learned</u> a lot about the way of life here.

2. Before I <u>came</u> here, I <u>had never bought</u> anything from a vending machine.

3. I <u>arrived</u> here only a short time ago. I <u>have been</u> here only since last Friday.

4. When I arrived here, I <u>didn't know</u> much about the United States. I <u>had seen</u> many movies about America, but that wasn't enough. **5.** My understanding of this country <u>has</u> changed a lot since I arrived. **6.** When I was in my country, I <u>coached</u> a children's soccer team. When I came here, I <u>wanted</u> to do the same thing. Now I am coaching a soccer team at a local elementary school. I <u>have been</u> coaching this team for the last two months. **7.** My grandfather <u>lived</u> in a small village in Italy when he was a child. At nineteen, he <u>moved</u> to Rome, where he <u>met</u> and <u>married</u> my grandmother in 1947. My father <u>was</u> born in Rome in 1950. I <u>was</u> born in Rome in 1979.

8. I <u>have been living</u> / <u>have lived</u> in my cousin's apartment since I <u>arrived</u> here. I <u>haven't been</u> able to find my own apartment yet. I <u>have looked</u> at several places for rent, but I <u>haven't found</u> one that I can afford. **9.** How long <u>have</u> you been living here? I <u>have</u> been here for almost two <u>years</u>. **10.** Why <u>haven't</u> you been in class the last couple of days?

~~~~~~~~~~~~~~~~~

~~~~~~~~~~~~~~~~~

Chapter Four: FUTURE TIME

EXERCISE 1, p. 51. *Simple future.*

6. weather'll　**7.** Mary'll　**8.** Bill'll　**9.** children'll　**10.** Who'll

11. Where'll　**12.** long'll　**13.** Nobody'll　**14.** That'll　**15.** What'll

EXERCISE 2, p. 52. WILL *vs.* BE GOING TO.

PART I. **2.** will be / is going to be . . . will come / is going to come　**3.** will probably see / am probably going to see　**4.** A: won't be / isn't going to be . . . Who will be / Who's going to be　B: will teach / is going to teach . . . will be / am going to be   **5.** will the damage we do to our environment today affect / is the damage we do to our environment today going to affect

PART II.   **8.** B: will do   C: will do   **9.** is going to erase   **10.** will meet
11. am going to meet   **12.** will get   **13.** am going to enroll . . . am going to take   **14.** will get   **15.** will go   **16.** am going to sell   **17.** will look

EXERCISE 3, p. 55. *Expressing the future in time clauses.*
   2. [After the rain <u>stops</u>,]   **3.** [before my wife <u>gets</u> home from work today.]
   4. [until Jessica <u>comes</u>.]   **5.** [As soon as the war <u>is</u> over,]   **6.** [when the tide <u>comes</u> in,]   **7.** [While I'<u>m driving</u> to work tomorrow,]

EXERCISE 4, p. 55. *Expressing the future in time clauses.*
   2. eat . . . will probably take / am probably going to take   **3.** get . . . will call / am going to call   **4.** watch . . . will write / am going to write   **5.** will wait / am going to wait . . . comes   **6.** stops . . . will walk / am going to walk   **7.** graduate . . . intend . . . will go . . . get   **8.** am going to listen . . . sleep   **9.** A: are you staying / are you going to stay   B: plan/am planning . . . hope/am hoping   A: will you do / are you going to do . . . leave   B: will return / am going to return . . . get   A: will be / am going to be . . . return . . . get

EXERCISE 6, p. 57.   *Using the present progressive and the simple present to express future time.*
   4. in the future   **5.** in the future   **6.** now   **7.** in the future   **8.** habitually
   9. in the future   **10.** in the future   **11.** habitually   **12.** A: now
   B: now   A: in the future   **13.** A: in the future   B: in the future   C: in the future   **14.** in the future   **15.** in the future   **16.** in the future
   17. in the future   **18.** in the future

EXERCISE 7, p. 59. *Using the present progressive to express future time.*
   Expected completions: **2.** am taking   **3.** are having . . . are coming
   4. am seeing   **5.** is going   **6.** are driving   **7.** is playing   **8.** am stopping

EXERCISE 10, p. 60. *Using the future progressive.*
   1. will be attending   **2.** arrive . . . will be waiting   **3.** get . . . will be shining . . . will be singing . . . will still be lying   **4.** B: will be lying   A: will be thinking   **5.** will be staying   **6.** will be doing . . . will be attending school . . . (will be) studying   **7.** is . . . will probably be raining   **8.** will be in

12

Chicago visiting   **9.** will be at the library working   **10.** will be living . . .
will be driving

EXERCISE 11, p. 62. *Perfect and perfect progressive tenses.*
1. have been . . . had been . . . will have been   **2.** get . . . will already have
arrived / will have already arrived   **3.** got . . . had already arrived
4. have been sitting . . . had been sitting . . . will have been sitting   **5.** will have
been driving [*also possible:* will have driven]   **6.** had been living / had lived . . .
will have been living / will have lived   **7.** get . . . will have taken   **8.** will
have been running   **9.** will have had . . . dies   **10.** will have been

EXERCISE 12, p. 63. *Review: future time.*
2. He will shave and shower, and then make a light breakfast.   **3.** After he eats
breakfast tomorrow, he will get ready to go to work.   **4.** By the time he gets to
work tomorrow, he will have drunk three cups of coffee.   **5.** Between 8:00 and
9:00, Bill will answer his e-mail and plan his day.   **6.** By 10:00 tomorrow, he
will have called his new clients.   **7.** At 11:00 tomorrow, Bill will be attending a
staff meeting.   **8.** He will go to lunch at noon and have a sandwich and a bowl of
soup.   **9.** After he finishes eating, he will take a short walk in the park before he
returns to the office.   **10.** He will work at his desk until he goes to another meeting
in the middle of the afternoon.   **11.** By the time he leaves the office, he will have
attended three meetings.   **12.** When Bill gets home, his children will be playing in
the yard.   **13.** They will have been playing since 3:00 in the afternoon.
14. As soon as he finishes dinner, he will take the children for a walk to a nearby
playground.   **15.** Afterward, the whole family will sit in the living room and
discuss their day.   **16.** They will watch television for a while, then Bill and his
wife will put the kids to bed.   **17.** By the time Bill goes to bed tomorrow, he will
have had a full day and will be ready for sleep.

~~~~~~~~~~~~~~~~~
~~~~~~~~~~~~~~~~~

Chapter Five: ADVERB CLAUSES OF TIME AND REVIEW OF VERB TENSES

EXERCISE 1, p. 65. *Error analysis: review of verb tenses.*

2. By the time I return to my country, I <u>will have been</u> away from home for more than three years. **3.** As soon as I ~~will~~ <u>graduate</u>, I <u>am</u> going to return to my hometown. **4.** By the end of the 21st century, scientists will <u>have</u> discovered the cure for the common cold. **5.** I want to get married, but I <u>haven't met</u> the right person yet. **6.** I have <u>seen</u> that movie three times, and now I <u>want</u> to see it again. **7.** Last night, I <u>had</u> dinner with two <u>friends</u>. I <u>have known</u> both of them for a long time. **8.** I <u>don't</u> like my job at the restaurant. My brother wants me to change it. I <u>think</u> he is right. **9.** So far this week, the teachers <u>have given</u> us a lot of homework every day. **10.** There <u>have been</u> more than forty presidents of the United States since it became a country. George Washington <u>was</u> the first president. He <u>became</u> the president in 1789. **11.** While I <u>am</u> studying tonight, I'm going to listen to Beethoven's Seventh Symphony. **12.** We washed the dishes and <u>cleaned</u> up the kitchen after our dinner guests <u>left/had left</u>. **13.** My neighbors are Mr. and Mrs. Jones. I <u>have known</u> them ever since I <u>was</u> a child. **14.** It <u>will rain</u> tomorrow morning. / It is <u>probably going to rain</u> tomorrow morning. **15.** Many scientists believe there <u>will be</u> / is <u>going to be</u> a major earthquake in California in the next few years. **16.** When I got home to my apartment last night, I <u>used</u> my key to open the door as usual. But the door didn't open. I <u>tried</u> my key again and again with no luck. So I <u>knocked</u> on the door for my wife to let me in. Finally the door <u>opened</u>, but I <u>didn't see</u> my wife on the other side. I saw a stranger. I had been <u>trying</u> to get into the wrong apartment! I quickly <u>apologized</u> and <u>went</u> to my own apartment.

EXERCISE 4, p. 68. *Review of verb tenses.*

1. is studying . . . is also taking . . . begin **2.** had already eaten . . . left . . . always eats . . . goes . . . goes . . . will eat/will have eaten **3.** called . . . was attending **4.** will be attending **5.** got . . . was sleeping . . . had been sleeping **6.** is taking . . . fell . . . has been sleeping **7.** started . . . hasn't finished . . . is reading **8.** has read . . . is reading . . . has been reading . . . intends . . . has read . . . has ever read **9.** eats . . . is going to go . . . will have eaten . . . goes

EXERCISE 6, p. 70. *Adverb clauses of time.*

Note: Adverb clauses are underlined.

1. We went inside <u>when it began to rain</u>. 2. It began to rain. We went inside.

3. <u>When it began to rain</u>, we went inside. 4. <u>When the mail comes</u>, my assistant opens it. 5. My assistant opens the mail <u>when it comes</u>. 6. The mail comes <u>around ten o'clock every morning</u>. My assistant opens it.

EXERCISE 7, p. 71. *Preview of Chart 5-2.*

Expected completions: 2. [after I <u>did</u> my homework.] 3. [after I <u>do</u> my homework.] 4. [Ever since I was a child,] I <u>have been</u> afraid of dogs.

5. [while she <u>was playing</u> basketball.] 6. [before you <u>hand</u> it in to the teacher tomorrow.] 7. [By the time I left my apartment this morning,] the mail carrier <u>had already delivered</u> the mail. 8. [since he <u>was</u> ten years old] 9. [as I <u>was driving</u> my car to work this morning.] 10. [By the time I leave this city,] I <u>will have been</u> here for four months. 11. [Whenever Mark <u>gets</u> angry,]

12. I <u>used to go</u> to the beach [whenever the weather was nice,] but now I don't have time to do that [because I have to study.] 13. [when <u>my parents arrive from Moscow</u>.] 14. [The next time I <u>go</u> to Hawaii,] 15. [the last time I <u>ate</u> at that restaurant]

EXERCISE 8, p. 73. *Using adverb clauses to show time relationships.*

3. Whenever/Every time Susan feels nervous, she chews her nails. (~~before~~)

4. The frying pan caught on fire while I was making dinner. (~~by the time,~~ ~~as soon as~~) 5. Someone knocked on the door just as we were sitting down to eat. Just after we sat down to eat, someone knocked on the door. (~~just before~~)

6. As soon as the singer finished her song, the audience burst into applause. The audience burst into applause immediately after the singer finished her song. (~~as long as~~) 7. We have to wait here until Nancy comes. (~~as soon as, after~~)

8. After / As soon as / When Nancy comes, we can leave for the theater. 9. I knew that something was wrong just as soon as/when my roommate walked into the room yesterday. (~~whenever~~) 10. Just before I stood up to give my speech, I got butterflies in my stomach. (~~until, while~~) 11. The first time I saw the great pyramids of Egypt in the moonlight, I was speechless. (~~until, before~~) 12. Jane has gotten three promotions since she started working at this company six months ago. (~~before, when~~) 13. The phone rang shortly after / not long after / a short time after I had gone to bed. 14. When/Once the weather gets warmer, we can start playing tennis again. (~~while~~) 15. By the time Shakespeare died in 1616, he had written more than 37 plays. (~~while, once~~) 16. The next time Sam goes to the movies, he'll remember to take his glasses. (~~as long as, by the time~~) 17. As long

as I live, I will not forget Mr. Tanaka. (~~as~~, ~~so long as~~) **18.** Mohammad had never heard about Halloween before/until he came to the U.S. (~~since~~)

EXERCISE 9, p. 74. *Verb tenses in adverb clauses of time.*

1. B	**2.** D	**3.** C	**4.** D	**5.** D	**6.** A	**7.** B
8. C	**9.** B	**10.** B	**11.** B	**12.** A	**13.** D	**14.** B

EXERCISE 11, p. 76. *Review of verb tenses.*

1. am listening **2.** A: Have you met B: have never had **3.** A: are you doing B: am trying A: will electrocute / are going to eletrocute **4.** A: is lying B: see . . . certainly looks **5.** A: went B: Was it A: enjoyed B: did you see A: had never seen B: have seen . . . saw . . . was . . . wasn't **6.** A: had never been B: were you doing A: were driving **7.** A: Are you taking B: am not A: Have you ever taken B: have A: did you take . . . was . . . is/was he B: is/was **8.** A: was . . . haven't received . . . don't have/haven't B: do you need A: will pay . . . get **9.** A: isn't B: will be sitting **10.** A: do you know . . . have been looking B: is seeing . . . received A: sounds . . . has . . . will be working

EXERCISE 12, p. 78. *Review of verb tenses.*

(1) Are you studying (2) am (3) have been . . . studied / was studying / had been studying (4) are you taking (5) am taking . . . are you taking (6) am studying . . . need . . . take (7) have you been (8) have been . . . arrived . . . have been studying . . . lived / was living (9) speak . . . Did you study / Had you studied . . . came (10) studied / had studied / had been studying . . . spent . . . picked . . . was living/lived (11) were . . . came . . . had never studied . . . started (12) do you plan / are you planning (13) I'm not . . . return . . . will have been (14) hope / am hoping

EXERCISE 13, p. 79. *Review of verb tenses.*

(1) received (2) have been trying . . . have been (3) have had (4) has been staying (5) and (6) have spent / have been spending (7) have been (8) went . . . watched (9) have barely had (10) is . . . am sitting (11) have been sitting (12) leaves . . . decided (13) am writing (14) am getting (15) will take / am going to take . . . get (16) are you getting (17) are your classes going

16

EXERCISE 15, p. 80. *Review of verb tenses.*

(1) has experienced   (2) will experience / is going to experience   (3) began
(4) have occurred   (5) causes   (6) have developed   (7) waves
(8) hold   (9) moves   (10) know   (11) happened   (12) struck
(13) were sitting   (14) suddenly found   (15) died . . . collapsed
(16) sent   (17) will the next earthquake occur / is the next earthquake going
to occur   (18) have often helped   (19) are studying   (20) and (21) also
appear   (22) seem   (23) have developed   (24) will be   (25) strikes

EXERCISE 19, p. 81. *Error analysis: general review.*

1. I <u>have been</u> living at 3371 **G**rand **A**venue since last September.   **2.** I have
been in New York **C**ity <u>for two weeks</u> ~~ago~~.   OR   I <u>was</u> in New York **C**ity two <u>weeks</u> ago.
3. My country <u>has changed</u> its capital city five <u>times</u>.   **4.** Dormitory life is not
quiet. Everyone <u>shouts</u> and <u>makes</u> a lot of noise in the halls.   **5.** My friends will
meet me when I ~~will~~ <u>arrive</u> at the airport.   **6.** Hasn't anyone ever <u>told</u> you to knock
on the door before you enter someone else's room? Didn't your parents <u>teach</u> you
that?   **7.** When I was a child, I viewed <u>things</u> from a much lower height. Many
physical objects around me <u>appeared</u> very large. When I <u>wanted</u> to move something
such as a chair, I <u>needed</u> help.   **8.** I ~~will~~ <u>intend</u> to go back home when I <u>finish</u> my
education.   **9.** The phone <u>rang</u> while I was doing the dishes. I <u>dried</u> my hands and
<u>answered</u> it. When I <u>heard</u> my <u>husband's</u> voice, I <u>was</u> very happy.   **10.** I <u>have</u>
<u>been</u> in the United States for the last four months. During this time, I <u>have</u> done
many <u>things</u> and <u>(have) seen</u> many <u>places</u>.   **11.** When the old man started to walk
back to his cave, the sun <u>had</u> already <u>hidden</u> itself behind the mountain.
12. While I <u>was</u> writing my composition last night, someone <u>knocked</u> on the door.
13. I'm <u>studying</u> English at an English conversation school two <u>times</u> a week.
14. Getting accustomed to a different <u>culture is</u> not easy.   **15.** I'm really glad you
<u>visited / are going to visit / will visit / will be visiting</u> my hometown this year.
16. While I was <u>visiting</u> my cousin in Los Angeles**,** we went to a Thai restaurant and
<u>ate</u> Thai food.   **17.** <u>After</u> we ate dinner**,** we watched TV.   OR   We ate dinner. We
watched TV <u>afterwards</u>.   **18.** When I was in my country, I <u>was</u> afraid to come to
the United States. I thought I couldn't walk outside at night because of the terrible
crime. But now I <u>have</u> a different opinion. I <u>have lived</u> in this small town for three
<u>months</u> and <u>(have) learned</u> that there is very little crime here.   **19.** Before I
came to the United <u>States</u>**,** I pictured the U.S. as an exciting place with <u>honest</u>**,** hard-
working, well-mannered <u>people</u>. <u>Since</u> I came to the United <u>States</u> four <u>months</u> ago**,**
this picture <u>has</u> changed. The manners of the students while [*also possible:* when]
they are in the cafeteria are really bad. I also <u>think</u> that office workers here <u>are</u> lazy.
People in my country <u>work</u> a lot harder.

Chapter Six: SUBJECT-VERB AGREEMENT

EXERCISE 1, p. 83. *Preview: using -S/-ES.*

2. works = *singular verb*   **3.** consists = *singular verb*   planets = *plural noun*   **4.** rotates = *singular verb*   **5.** animals = *plural noun*   **6.** needs = *singular verb*   **7.** Students, tests = *plural nouns*   **8.** wings = *plural noun*   **9.** Swallows, creatures = *plural nouns*   **10.** Butterflies = *plural noun*   **11.** sunsets = *plural noun*   **12.** contains = *singular verb*   books = *plural noun*   **13.** Encyclopedias, things = *plural nouns*   **14.** watches = *singular verb*   **15.** changes = *singular verb*

EXERCISE 2, p. 85. *Pronunciation of final -S/-ES.*

GROUP A.

2. feeds /z/   **3.** hates /s/   **4.** lids /z/   **5.** sleep /s/   **6.** robs /z/   **7.** trips /s/   **8.** grabs /z/   **9.** wishes /əz/   **10.** matches /əz/   **11.** guesses /əz/

GROUP B.

12. books /s/   **13.** homes /z/   **14.** occurs /z/   **15.** fixes /əz/
16. sizes /əz/   **17.** pages /əz/   **18.** unlocks /s/   **19.** fills /z/
20. ashes /əz/   **21.** sniffs /s/   **22.** miles /z/   **23.** rugs /z/

GROUP C.

24. arranges /əz/   **25.** itches /əz/   **26.** relaxes /əz/   **27.** rises /əz/
28. laughs /s/   **29.** days /z/   **30.** pies /z/   **31.** agrees /z/
32. faces /əz/   **33.** quizzes /əz/   **34.** judges /əz/   **35.** asks /s/

EXERCISE 3, p. 85. *Spelling of final -S/-ES.*

3. talks /s/   **4.** blushes /əz/   **5.** discovers /z/   **6.** develops /s/
7. seasons /z/   **8.** flashes /əz/   **9.** halls /z/   **10.** touches /əz/
11. coughs /s/   **12.** presses /əz/   **13.** methods /z/   **14.** mixes /əz/
15. tries /z/   **16.** trays /z/   **17.** enemies /z/   **18.** guys /z/

EXERCISE 5, p. 86. *Pronunciation of final -S/-ES.*

1. encourage/əz/ . . . student/s/   2. chicken/z/, duck/s/ . . . turkey/z/ . . . egg/z/   3. possess/əz/ . . . quality/z/   4. wage/əz/ . . . tax/əz/   5. serve/z/ . . . sandwich/əz/   6. cough/s/, sneeze/əz/ . . . wheeze/əz/   7. shape/s/ . . . size/əz/   8. practice/əz/ . . . sentence/əz/   9. shirt/s/, shoe/z/, sock/s/, dress/əz/, slack/s/, blouse/əz/, earring/z/ . . . necklace/əz/   [*Note: "slacks" has no singular form; there is no such thing as "one slack."*]   10. scratch/əz/ . . . itch/əz/

EXERCISE 6, p. 87. *Use of final -S/-ES.*

1. A stamp collector collects stamps.   2. An animal trainer trains animals.   3. A bank robber robs banks.   4. A dog catcher catches dogs.   5. A book publisher publishes books.   6. A tax collector collects taxes.   7. A ticket taker takes tickets.   8. A fire extinguisher extinguishes fires.   9. A mind reader reads minds.   10. A bullfighter fights bulls.   11. A wage earner earns wages.   12. A storyteller tells stories.

EXERCISE 7, p. 87. *Use of final -S/-ES.*

Possible responses: 1. A baby cries / eats / sleeps.   2. A telephone rings.   3. A star shines / twinkles.   4. A dog barks / runs / fetches.   5. A duck quacks / swims.   6. A ball bounces / rolls.   7. A heart beats / pounds / races / pumps.   8. A river flows / overflows / dries up.   9. A cat purrs / chases mice.   10. A door closes / shuts / opens / swings.   11. A clock ticks / chimes / tells time.   12. An airplane flies / lands / takes off.   13. A doctor heals / sees patients / prescribes medicine.   14. A teacher teaches / instructs / educates / gives homework.   15. A psychologist studies human behavior / helps people with problems.

EXERCISE 8, p. 87. *Preview: subject-verb agreement.*

2. gets   3. are   4. is   5. is   6. are   7. is   8. are   9. is   10. is   11. are   12. has   13. has   14. was/were   15. is   16. speak   17. are [*also possible, but very informal and substandard:* is]   18. is   19. is   20. is   21. is   22. like   23. are   24. is   25. have   26. are   27. works   28. are   29. is   30. is

EXERCISE 9, p. 89. *Subject-verb agreement.*

1. astounds   2. are   3. is   4. are   5. agree   6. approves   7. has   8. is   9. is   10. was   11. do   12. were   13. Is   14. has

EXERCISE 10, p. 90. *Using expressions of quantity.*

1. is **2.** are **3.** are **4.** is **5.** are **6.** is **7.** is **8.** has
9. has **10.** is **11.** is/are . . . are **12.** are **13.** is **14.** is
15. Do **16.** Does **17.** were **18.** was **19.** is **20.** is
21. Do [*Note: Approximately 70% of the earth's surface is covered by water.*]

EXERCISE 11, p. 91. *Using* THERE *and* BE.

1. aren't **2.** isn't **3.** are **4.** is **5.** are **6.** are **7.** isn't
8. was **9.** is **10.** are **11.** has been **12.** have been

EXERCISE 13, p. 93. *Irregularities in subject-verb agreement.*

1. has **2.** is **3.** is **4.** seeks **5.** is **6.** are **7.** is
8. is **9.** is **10.** do **11.** are **12.** is **13.** are **14.** is
15. commute **16.** is . . . isn't **17.** are **18.** depends . . are . . . have

EXERCISE 14, p. 93. *Review: subject-verb agreement.*

1. is **2.** are **3.** are **4.** is **5.** is **6.** are **7.** is **8.** is
9. is **10.** is **11.** are **12.** is **13.** is **14.** are **15.** are
16. is **17.** are **18.** is **19.** is **20.** are **21.** is **22.** is
23. are **24.** is **25.** is **26.** are **27.** are **28.** is/are
29. are **30.** is **31.** are **32.** are **33.** is **34.** are **35.** is

EXERCISE 15, p. 94. *Error analysis: subject-verb agreement.*

3. All of the employees in that company <u>are</u> required to be proficient in a second language. **4.** A lot of the people in my class <u>work</u> during the day and <u>attend</u> class in the evening. **5.** Listening to very loud music at rock concerts <u>has</u> caused hearing loss in some teenagers. **6.** Many of the satellites orbiting the earth <u>are</u> used for communications. **7.** *(no errors)* **8.** Chinese <u>has</u> more than fifty thousand written characters. **9.** About two-thirds of the Vietnamese <u>work</u> in agriculture. **10.** *(no errors)* **11.** *(no errors)* **12.** *(no errors)* **13.** Every girl and boy <u>is</u> required to have certain immunizations before enrolling in public school. **14.** Seventy-five percent of the people in New York City <u>live</u> in upstairs apartments, not on the ground floor. **15.** Unless there <u>is</u> a profound and extensive reform of government policies in the near future, the economic conditions in that country will continue to deteriorate. **16.** While I was in Paris, some of the best food I found <u>was</u> not at the well-known eating places, but in small out-of-the-way cafes. **17.** <u>Where are</u> my gloves? Have you seen them anywhere? I can't find them. **18.** *(no errors)* **19.** *(no errors)* OR *[possible but extremely formal:* are] **20.** *(no errors)* **21.** Studying a foreign language

often <u>leads</u> students to learn about the culture of the <u>country</u> where it is spoken.
22. *(no errors)* **23.** Some of the <u>movies</u> about ~~the~~ gangsters <u>are</u> surprisingly funny. **24.** *(no errors)* **25.** How many people <u>are</u> there in Canada?
26. *(no errors)* **27.** Which one of the continents in the world <u>is</u> uninhabited? [*answer:* Antarctica] **28.** One of the most common names for dogs in the United States <u>is</u> Rover. **29.** Everybody in my family <u>enjoys</u> music and reading.
30. Most of the mountain peaks in the Himalayan Range <u>are</u> covered with snow the year round.

EXERCISE 16, p. 96. *Review: subject-verb agreement.*

2. are   3. keeps   4. makes   5. is   6. is   7. Does   8. Do
9. is   10. are   11. are   12. Are   13. is   14. beats
15. provides   16. oversimplifies   17. is   18. plan   19. concerns
20. is   21. is   22. appears   23. are   24. is   25. speaks

~~~~~~~~~~~~~~~~~
~~~~~~~~~~~~~~~~~

Chapter Seven: NOUNS

EXERCISE 1, p. 99. *Preview: plural nouns.*

3. mice   4. monkeys   5. industries   6. women   7. foxes
8. geese   9. sheep   10. series   11. beliefs   12. leaves
13. selves   14. echoes   15. photos   16. analyses   17. hypotheses
18. curricula   19. phenomena   20. stimuli   21. offspring
22. bacteria

EXERCISE 2, p. 101. *Plural nouns.*

3. teeth   4. boxes . . . oxen   5. mice   6. beaches . . . cliffs   7. leaves
8. attorneys   9. discoveries . . . laboratories   10. fish   11. wolves,
foxes, deer . . . sheep   12. echoes   13. pianos   14. phenomena   15. media

EXERCISE 3, p. 102. *Plural nouns.*

(1) Bacteria . . . things . . . organisms   (2) Bacteria . . . bodies . . . creatures
(3) thousands . . . kinds . . . bacteria   (4) Viruses . . . organisms . . . viruses . . .
cells . . . things . . . particles . . . hundreds . . . times   (5) Viruses . . . diseases . . .
beings . . . illnesses   (6) Viruses   (7) officials . . . conditions
(8) officials . . . infections . . . bacteria . . . forms   (9) infections . . .
infections . . . doctors

EXERCISE 4, p. 103. *Possessive nouns.*

2. boy's   **3.** boys'   **4.** children's   **5.** child's   **6.** baby's
7. babies'   **8.** wives'   **9.** wife's   **10.** Sally's   **11.** Phyllis's/Phyllis'
12. boss's   **13.** bosses'   **14.** woman's   **15.** women's   **16.** sister's
17. sisters'   **18.** yesterday's   **19.** today's   **20.** month's

EXERCISE 5, p. 104. *Possessive nouns.*

3. father's   **4.** I have four aunts. All of my aunts' homes . . . mother's
5. aunt's   **6.** Five astronauts were . . . The astronauts' safe return
7. children's   **8.** child's   **9.** secretary's   **10.** people's   **11.** Bill's
12. Bess's/Bess'   **13.** Quite a few diplomats are . . . Almost all of the diplomats'
children   **14.** diplomat's

EXERCISE 6, p. 104. *Using apostrophes.*

2. bear's   **3.** It's . . . world's   **4.** individual's   **5.** heroes' . . . hero's
6. Children's . . . they're . . . Adults' toys . . . children's toys

EXERCISE 7, p. 105. *Using nouns as modifiers.*

2. flowers . . . flower   **3.** beans . . . bean   **4.** babies . . . baby
5. children . . . child   **6.** salads . . . salad   **7.** faxes . . . fax   **8.** cans . . .
can . . . potatoes . . . potato   **9.** airplanes . . . Airplane   **10.** mosquitoes . . .
mosquito   **11.** two-hour . . . two hours   **12.** ten years old . . . ten-year-old
13. ten . . . speeds . . . ten-speed   **14.** six games . . . six-game
15. three-letter . . . three letters

EXERCISE 8, p. 107. *Using nouns as modifiers.*

Possible responses: **1.** a cotton shirt, cotton balls   **2.** a grammar book, a
grammar test   **3.** a birthday card, a birthday present   **4.** chicken salad,
chicken soup   **5.** an airplane trip, an airplane ticket   **6.** a telephone book, a
telephone call   **7.** a mountain peak, a mountain climber   **8.** a government
official, a government program   **9.** a football game, a football uniform

10. a bedroom table, bedroom slippers   11. a silk scarf, a silk blouse
12. a morning newspaper, a morning meeting   13. a street sign, a street light
14. a newspaper headline, a newspaper article   15. an hotel lobby, an hotel room
16. a kitchen table, a kitchen sink   17. baby food, a baby bottle
18. vegetable soup, a vegetable brush   19. an office building, an office party
20. a bicycle tire, a bicycle lane

EXERCISE 9, p. 107. *Count and noncount nouns.*
2. jewelry (NC) . . . rings (C) . . . bracelets (C) . . . necklace (C)   3. mountains
(C) . . . fields (C) . . . lakes (C) . . . scenery (NC)   4. Gold (NC) . . . iron (NC)
5. iron (C)   6. baseball (NC) . . . baseball (C)

EXERCISE 10, p. 109. *Count and noncount nouns.*
3. music   4. traffic   5. garbage   6. junk   7. stuff   8. thunder
9. screwdrivers   10. hardware   11. homework   12. luggage/baggage
13. this information   14. advice   15. progress

EXERCISE 11, p. 110. *Count and noncount nouns; nouns as modifiers.*
Only corrections are included in the answers: 3. trees, bushes . . . flowers
4. suggestions   5. words   6. glasses   7. windows   8. glasses
9. assignments   10. (three) times   11. typewriters, copiers, telephones . . .
staplers   12. substances   13. novels . . . essays . . . poets . . . poems
14. seasons   15. rewards   16. machines . . . (Modern) factories (need)
17. travelers . . . suitcases . . . days . . . months   18. magazines, envelopes . . .
boxes . . . books . . . bottles, jars . . . cans   19. stars . . . grains

EXERCISE 12, p. 113. *Article usage with generic nouns.*
4. A concert   5. An opera   6. Ø   7. A cup   8. Ø   9. An island
10. Ø   11. A bridge   12. A valley   13. Ø   14. An adjective
15. Ø   16. Ø   17. A (tennis) player   18. A tree   19. Ø
20. Ø   21. Ø   22. A sentence   23. Ø   24. Ø   25. An
orange   26. Ø   27. Ø   28. An iron   29. A basketball   30. Ø

EXERCISE 13, p. 113. *Article usage with indefinite nouns.*
5. an accident   6. some homework   7. a table   8. some furniture
9. some chairs   10. some advice   11. a suitcase   12. some luggage
13. an earthquake   14. some letters   15. a letter   16. some mail
17. a machine   18. some new machinery   19. Some machines
20. some junk   21. an old basket   22. some old boots

EXERCISE 15, p. 115. *Article usage.*

3. a good reason   **4.** the reason   **5.** the washing machine . . . a different shirt
6. a washing machine   **7.** A: The radiator . . . a leak . . . the windshield wipers
B: the leak   **8.** A: The front wheel   B: a parked car . . . a big pothole
A: the car   B: a note . . . the owner . . . the car   A: the note   B: an apology
9. the closet . . . the front hallway

EXERCISE 16, p. 116. *Article usage.*

4. ∅   **5.** A hat . . . an article   **6.** ∅ . . . ∅   **7.** The brown hat
8. ∅ . . . ∅   **9.** a long life   **10.** the life   **11.** an engineer   **12.** an
engineer   **13.** the name . . . the engineer . . . an infection . . . the bridge
14. ∅ . . . ∅   **15.** The jewelry

EXERCISE 17, p. 117. *Article usage.*

1 . a new phone   **2.** the phone   **3.** ∅ . . . ∅ . . . ∅ . . . ∅ . . . ∅ . . . ∅
4. a sandy shore . . . ∅ . . . the surface . . . ∅ . . . ∅, ∅, ∅, ∅ . . . ∅ . . . ∅
5 . the sand . . . ∅ . . . a crab . . . The crab . . . a good time . . . the beach
6 . ∅, ∅ . . . ∅ . . . a person   **7.** ∅ . . . ∅ . . . the universe   **8.** ∅ . . . ∅ . . . a
thin layer . . . ∅ . . . ∅   **9.** a recent newspaper article . . . an Australian swimmer
. . . a shark . . . a group . . . the shark . . . the swimmer . . . the dolphins . . . the
swimmer's life   **10.** ∅ . . . ∅ . . . ∅ . . . an average . . . ∅   **11.** ∅ . . . ∅
12. a fly . . . the ceiling . . . the fly . . . the ceiling

EXERCISE 18, p. 118. *Preview: expressions of quantity.*

1. i. ~~too much~~   **2.** a. ~~two~~   h. ~~too many~~
k. ~~a little~~   b. ~~a couple of~~   j. ~~a few~~
m. ~~a great deal of~~   c. ~~both~~   l. ~~a number of~~
d. ~~several~~

EXERCISE 19, p. 119. *Expressions of quantity.*

1. b. ~~several~~   g. ~~a few~~   **2.** e. ~~too much~~
f. ~~too many~~   i. ~~a number of~~   h. ~~a little~~
j. ~~a great deal of~~

EXERCISE 20, p. 120. MUCH *vs.* MANY.

3. much mail   **4.** many letters   **5.** aren't many hotels   **6.** is too much
furniture   **7.** isn't much traffic   **8.** aren't many cars   **9.** much work
10. many sides   **11.** much information   **12.** much homework

13. many people   14. much postage   15. is too much violence
16. much patience   17. many patients   18. many teeth   19. isn't much
international news   20. many fish are   21. many continents are
22. much progress

EXERCISE 21, p. 121. *Expressions of quantity.*
   4. Ø . . . loaves of bread . . . Ø . . . jars of honey   5. novels . . . Ø . . . poems . . . Ø
   6. orange juice . . . light bulbs . . . hardware . . . computer software   7. sleep . . .
information . . . facts . . . help   8. women . . . movies . . . scenes . . . Ø
   9. shirts . . . Ø . . . pens . . . Ø   10. patience . . . wealth . . . Ø . . . Ø
   11. luck . . . money . . . advice . . . Ø   12. ideas . . . theories . . . hypotheses . . . Ø

EXERCISE 22, p. 122. *Expressions of quantity.*
   1. much furniture   2. many desks   3. many branches   4. much equipment
   5. much machinery   6. many machines   7. many women   8. many pieces
   9. many mice   10. much advice   11. many sheep   12. much
homework   13. many prizes   14. many geese   15. much music
   16. much progress   17. many races   18. much knowledge   19. many
marriages   20. much information   21. much luck   22. many
hypotheses   23. much mail   24. many offices   25. much slang
   26. many roofs   27. many shelves   28. many teeth

EXERCISE 23, p. 123. *Using* A FEW *and* FEW; A LITTLE *and* LITTLE.
   3. a little sunshine   4. very little sunshine   5. a few programs   6. very few
television programs   7. a few drops   8. a little oil   9. very little jewelry

EXERCISE 24, p. 124. *Using* A FEW *and* FEW; A LITTLE *and* LITTLE.
   3. a little salt   4. very little salt   5. a little music   6. very little traffic
   7. very few friends   8. a few days . . . a few days   9. a few more minutes
   10. a little more time   11. a few nuts   12. very few toys   13. a little rain
   14. a little honey . . . a little milk   15. very little patience   16. very few
problems

EXERCISE 25, p. 125. *Using* OF *in expressions of quantity.*
   3. Ø . . . Ø   4. of   5. Ø   6. of   7. Ø   8. of   9. Ø
   10. of   11. Ø   12. of   13. of   14. of   15. Ø   16. of
   17. Ø . . . of   18. Ø   19. of   20. Ø

EXERCISE 26, p. 126. ALL (OF) *and* BOTH (OF).

   3. (of)   **4.** Ø   **5.** Ø   **6.** Ø . . . Ø . . . (of)   **7.** (of)   **8.** (of)
   9. (of)   **10.** Ø . . . Ø

EXERCISE 27, p. 127. *Using* OF *in expressions of quantity.*

   4. Ø   **5.** of   **6.** of   **7.** Ø . . . Ø . . . Ø   **8.** of   **9.** Ø . . . Ø
   10. of . . . of   **11.** Ø   **12.** Ø . . . of

EXERCISE 28, p. 128. *Using* ONE, EACH, *and* EVERY.

   2. girls   **3.** children   **4.** child   **5.** member   **6.** members

EXERCISE 29, p. 129. *Using* ONE, EACH, *and* EVERY.

   3. countries   **4.** each student / each of the students   **5.** *(no change)*
   6. All (of) the furniture / Each piece of furniture   **7.** Some of the equipment /
One piece of equipment / One of the pieces of equipment   **8.** each woman / each
of the women / all of the women   **9.** places   **10.** *(no change)*   **11.** language
   12. each of the errors / each error

~~~~~~~~~~~~~~~~~
~~~~~~~~~~~~~~~~~

Chapter Eight: PRONOUNS

EXERCISE 1, p. 131. *Preview: personal pronouns.*

   1. Some North American food is very good, but I don't like most of <u>it</u>.   **2.** When we
were schoolgirls, my sister and <u>I</u> used to play badminton after school every day.
   3. If you want to pass <u>your</u> exams, you had better study very hard for <u>them</u>.
   4. The work had to be finished by my boss and <u>me</u> after the store had closed for the
night.   **5.** A hippopotamus spends most of <u>its</u> time in the water of rivers and lakes.
   6. After work, Mr. Gray asked to speak to Tim and <u>me</u> about the company's new
policies. He explained <u>them</u> to us and asked for <u>our</u> opinions.   **7.** <u>Children</u> should
learn to respect other people. They need to learn how to treat other people

politely, including their playmates.   **8.** My friends asked to borrow my car because <u>theirs</u> was in the garage for repairs.

EXERCISE 2, p. 132. *Personal pronouns: antecedents.*

2. they . . . they = *pronouns;* monkeys = *antecedent*   **3.** She = *pronoun;* teacher = *antecedent*   them = *pronoun;* papers = *antecedent*   **4.** her . . . She = *pronouns* ; Nancy = *antecedent*   it = *pronoun;* apple = *antecedent*   **5.** it = *pronoun* ; dog = *antecedent*   **6.** She . . . She = *pronouns;* cat = *antecedent* His . . . him = *pronouns;* Tom = *antecedent*   They = *pronoun;* dogs = *antecedent* him = *pronoun* ;Tom = *antecedent*

EXERCISE 3, p. 133. *Possessive pronouns and adjectives.*

2. mine . . . yours   **3.** their books . . . hers . . . his   **4.** its   **5.** It's true . . . its way . . . its trip   **6.** Its name . . . It's a turtle . . . It's been (It's been = It has been)   **7.** Our house . . . Our neighbor's house . . . ours . . . theirs   **8.** It . . . its prey . . . its long, pointed bill . . . it . . . it . . . it . . . It's interesting . . . them

EXERCISE 4, p. 134. *Personal pronoun use with generic nouns.*

3. <u>Students</u> in Biology 101 <u>have</u> to spend three hours per week in the laboratory, where <u>they do</u> various experiments by following the directions in <u>their</u> lab <u>manuals</u>. **4.** <u>Pharmacists fill</u> prescriptions, but <u>they are</u> not allowed to prescribe medicine. **5.** *(no change)*   **6.** <u>Citizens</u> have two primary responsibilties. <u>They</u> should vote in every election, and <u>they</u> should serve willingly on a jury.   **7.** *(no change)* **8.** <u>Lecturers need</u> to prepare <u>their</u> notes carefully so that <u>they do</u> not lost <u>their</u> place while <u>they are</u> delivering <u>their</u> speech.

EXERCISE 5, p. 135. *Personal pronoun use with indefinite pronouns.*

2. s/he wants; he or she wants; they want   **3.** his/her; their   **4.** his/her; their   **5.** anyone; his/her; their   **6.** him/her; them   **7.** s/he . . . his/her; they . . . their   **8.** s/he pleases; they please

EXERCISE 6, p. 136. *Personal pronoun use with collective nouns.*

2. it consists   **3.** It   **4.** They   **5.** they   **6.** It doesn't   **7.** they **8.** It was   **9.** They are . . . their . . . them   **10.** It is

EXERCISE 8, p. 137. *Preview of reflexive pronouns.*

2. himself   **3.** herself   **4.** themselves   **5.** ourselves   **6.** yourself **7.** yourselves   **8.** oneself

EXERCISE 9, p. 138. *Reflexive pronouns.*

2. herself **3.** themselves **4.** herself **5.** yourself . . . himself . . . myself . . . ourselves . . . themselves **6.** myself **7.** himself **8.** yourself **9.** themselves **10.** herself

EXERCISE 10, p. 139. *Reflexive pronouns.*

2. enjoy himself **3.** proud of yourselves **4.** pat yourself **5.** killed himself **6.** entertained themselves **7.** introduced myself **8.** feeling sorry for yourself **9.** talking to yourself **10.** laugh at ourselves **11.** promised herself **12.** angry at himself

EXERCISE 12, p. 141. *Review of nouns and pronouns, singular and plural.*

2. Millions of years ago, they had wings. These wings changed as the birds adapted to their environment. **3.** Penguins' principal food was fish. Penguins needed to be able to swim to find their food, so eventually their wings evolved into flippers that enabled them to swim through water with speed and ease. **4.** Penguins spend most of their lives in water. However, they lay their eggs on land. **5.** Emperor penguins have interesting egg-laying habits. **6.** The female lays one egg on the ice in Arctic regions, and then immediately returns to the ocean. **7.** After the female lays the egg, the male takes over. He covers the egg with his body until it hatches. **8.** This process takes seven to eight weeks. During this time, the male doesn't eat. **9.** After the egg hatches, the female returns to take care of the chick, and the male goes to the ocean to find food for himself, his mate, and their offspring. **10.** Although the penguins' natural habitat is in polar regions, we can see them in most major zoos in the world. They seem to adapt well to life in confinement, so we can enjoy watching their antics without feeling sorry about their loss of freedom.

EXERCISE 13, p. 143. *Using* OTHER.

2. Another . . . Another . . . Another . . . the other **3.** The other **4.** The others **5.** The other **6.** others **7.** other **8.** another **9.** Others **10.** the other **11.** other **12.** others **13.** another **14.** another **15.** Another . . . Others **16.** others **17.** Another . . . Others . . . other **18.** the other **19.** the others **20.** another **21.** Another . . . The other

EXERCISE 15, p. 145. *Using* OTHER.

2. Another . . . other **3.** one another / each other **4.** the other **5.** other . . . other **6.** other **7.** others . . . others . . . other **8.** each

other / one another another . . . each other / one another . . . each other / one another
. . . other   **9.** other   **10.** other   **11.** another

EXERCISE 17, p. 147. *Summary review.*

1. That book <u>contains</u> many different <u>kinds</u> of <u>stories</u> and <u>articles</u>.   **2.** ~~The~~ English
is one of the most important <u>languages</u> in the world.   **3.** She is always willing to
help her friends in every possible <u>way</u>.   **4.** In the past, horses <u>were</u> the principal
<u>means</u> of transportation.   **5.** He succeeded in creating one of the best <u>armies</u> in the
world.   **6.** There <u>is much equipment</u> in the research laboratory, but
undergraduates are not allowed to use <u>it</u>.   **7.** All of the <u>guests</u> enjoyed <u>themselves</u>
at the reception.   **8.** I have a <u>five-year-old</u> daughter and a <u>three-year-old</u> son.
9. Each <u>state</u> in the country <u>has</u> a different language.   **10.** Most of <u>the</u> people/
Most ~~of~~ people in my apartment building <u>are</u> friendly.   **11.** A political leader
should have the ability to adapt <u>himself/herself</u> to a changing world.   **12.** In my
opinion, ~~an~~ international <u>students</u> should live in a dormitory because they will meet
many people and can practice their English every day. Also, if <u>they</u> live in a
dormitory, <u>their</u> food is provided for <u>them</u>.   **13.** When I lost my passport, I had to
apply for ~~the~~ another one.   **14.** When I got to class, all of the <u>other</u> students were
already in their seats.   **15.** Everyone <u>seeks</u> ~~the~~ happiness in their <u>lives</u>. OR
Everyone <u>seeks</u> ~~the~~ happiness in <u>his/her</u> life.   **16.** In my country, there <u>are</u> a <u>lot</u>
of schools / ~~a~~ lots of schools.   **17.** Writing compositions <u>is</u> very hard for me.
18. It's difficult for me to understand English when people <u>use</u> a lot of <u>slang</u>.
19. ~~A~~ <u>Students</u> at the university should attend class regularly and hand in their
assignments on time. OR A student at the university should attend classes regularly
and hand in <u>his/her</u> assignments on time.   **20.** In my opinion, ~~the~~ <u>English</u> is <u>an</u>
easy language to learn.

EXERCISE 18, p. 148. *Summary review.*

1. There <u>are</u> many different <u>kinds</u> of <u>animals</u> in the world.   **2.** My cousin and her
husband want to move to <u>another</u> city because they don't like ~~a~~ cold weather.
3. I like to travel because I like to learn about other <u>countries</u> and <u>customs</u>.
4. Collecting stamps is one of my <u>hobbies</u>.   **5.** I came here three and a half <u>months</u>
ago. I think I have made ~~a~~ good progress in English.   **6.** I was looking for my
keys, but I couldn't find <u>them</u>.   **7.** When my mother was <u>a</u> child, she lived in a
small town. Now this town is <u>a</u> big city with tall <u>buildings</u> and many <u>highways</u>.
8. English has borrowed quite a few ~~of~~ <u>words</u> from <u>other</u> languages.   **9.** There
<u>are</u> many <u>students</u> from <u>different</u> countries in this class.   **10.** <u>Thousands</u> of
<u>athletes</u> take part in the Olympics.   **11.** Education is one of the most important
<u>aspects</u> of life. <u>Knowledge</u> about many different things <u>allows</u> us to live fuller lives.

12. All of the <u>students'</u> names were on the list.   **13.** I live in a <u>two-room</u> apartment.   **14.** Many <s>of</s> people prefer to live in small towns. Their attachment to their communities <u>prevents</u> them from moving from place to place in search of <u>work</u>.
15. <u>Today's</u> news is just as bad as <u>yesterday's</u> news.   **16.** Almost <u>all</u> of the students / Almost <u>all</u> <s>of</s> the students in our class <u>speak</u> English well.   **17.** The teacher gave us <u>some</u> homework to hand in next Tuesday.   **18.** Today <u>women</u> work as <u>doctors</u>, <u>pilots</u>, <u>archeologists</u>, and many other <u>things</u>. Both my mother and father are <u>teachers</u>.   **19.** Every <u>employee</u> in our company <u>respects</u> Mr. Ward.
20. <u>Children need </u>to learn how to get along with <u>other</u> people, how to spend <u>their</u> time wisely, and how to depend on <u>themselves</u>. [Also possible, but more stylistically awkward in its use of pronouns: A child needs to learn how to get along with <u>other</u> people, how to spend his or her time wisely, and how to depend on <u>himself or herself</u>]

~~~~~~~~~~~~~~~~~~~~
~~~~~~~~~~~~~~~~~~~~

Chapter Nine: MODALS, Part 1

EXERCISE 1, p. 152. *Forms of modals.*
   1-4. She can see it.   **5.** Can you please <s>to</s> pass the rice?   **6.** Can you see it?
   7. They can't go there.

EXERCISE 3, p. 154. *Polite requests with* WOULD YOU MIND.
   3. mailing   **4.** if I stayed   **5.** opening/if I opened   **6.** if I asked
   7. if I smoked   **8.** speaking   **9.** if I changed/changing   **10.** if I borrowed

EXERCISE 5, p. 155. *Polite requests.*
Possible completions: **2.** Could we have a few more minutes?   **3.** Could I get a ride with you?   **4.** Would you mind meeting Wednesday instead?   **5.** Could you take a look at them?   **6.** May I help you? . . . Could I see what you have in silk scarves?   **7.** Would you mind changing seats / if we changed seats?   **8.** May I call you this evening?

EXERCISE 9, p. 158. HAVE TO *and* MUST *in the negative.*
   3. don't have to   **4.** must not   **5.** doesn't have to   **6.** must not

7. don't have to   8. don't have to   9. must not   10. don't have to
11. must not   12. doesn't have to\

EXERCISE 12, p. 161. SHOULD, OUGHT TO, HAD BETTER.
Sample completions: **2.** hurt my feet . . . return them.   **3.** finish your
homework . . . forbid you to watch TV tonight.   **4.** put anitfreeze in the car
5. be ready for the test . . . I don't feel confident.   **6.** help us with dinner . . .
We'd be happy to help. Shall I set the table?   **7.** give up caffeine, but I love coffee
. . . listen to your doctor.   **8.** call your brother if you want him to pick you up at
the airport next week . . . do that now.   **9.** finished your report yet? . . . do it soon.
10. swim . . . a lifeguard? . . . ask him to teach Mary how to swim.   **11.** study or
go to a movie? . . . study . . . you won't be prepared for class tomorrow.   **12.** tired
all the time . . . see a doctor . . . seeing an acupuncturist?

EXERCISE 13, p. 162. *Necessity, advisability, and prohibition.*
The stronger sentence in each pair: **1.** b.   **2.** b.   **3.** a.   **4.** a.
5. b.   **6.** a.

EXERCISE 14, p. 162. SHOULD *vs.* MUST/HAVE TO.
3. must / have to   **4.** have to / must [*Note: "have to" is preferable here
because the situation is neither formal nor urgent.*]   **5.** should   **6.** should
7. should / must / have to [*if it's a requirement*]   **8.** must   **9.** should
10. must [*spoken with enthusiasm and emphasis*]

EXERCISE 15, p. 163. *The past form of* SHOULD.
1. He/She shouldn't have left the door open.   **2.** I should have gone to the meeting.
3. (. . .) should have gone to see a doctor.   **4.** (. . .) shouldn't have sold his/her
car.   **5.** (. . .) should have read the contact more carefully.

EXERCISE 16, p. 164. *The past form of* SHOULD.
Expected responses: **1.** I should have worn a coat.   **2.** I should have looked the
word up in the dictionary.   **3.** I should have written my friend a letter.
4. I shouldn't have spent my money foolishly.   **5.** I shouldn't have opened the
window.   **6.** I should have gone to the grocery store.   **7.** I should have set
my alarm clock.   **8.** I should have gone to (New Orleans) with my friends.
9. I should have had a cup fo coffee.   **10.** John should have married Mary.
11. John shouldn't have married Mary.   **12.** I should have stayed home
yesterday.   **13.** I should have gone outside and enjoyed the nice weather.
14. I should have bought my girlfriend/boyfriend a different present.

15. The little girl shouldn't have told a lie / should have told the truth.

16. I should not have lent (. . .) my car.

EXERCISE 18, p. 166. *Error analysis:* BE SUPPOSED TO.

1. The building custodian <u>is</u> supposed to unlock the classrooms every morning.

2. We're not <u>supposed</u> to open that door.   **3.** Where are we <u>supposed</u> to meet?

4. I have a meeting at seven tonight. I <u>am supposed</u> to be there a little early to discuss the agenda.   **5.** When we go to the store, Annie, you <u>are</u> not <u>supposed</u> to handle the glassware. It might break, and then you'd have to pay for it out of your allowance.   **6.** I'm <u>supposed</u> to be at the meeting. I suppose I'd better go.

7. Where have you been? You <u>were supposed</u> to be here an hour ago!

8. A: I can't remember what the boss said. <u>Am</u> I supposed to work in the mail order room tomorrow morning and then the shipping department tomorrow afternoon? Or the other way around?   B: How am I <u>supposed</u> to remember what you <u>are supposed</u> to do? I have enough trouble remembering what I <u>am</u> supposed <u>to do</u> / <u>am</u> supposed <u>to be doing</u>.

EXERCISE 20, p. 167. Necessity, advisability, and expectations.

The stronger sentence in each pair:

1. a.   **2.** a.   **3.** a.   **4.** a.   **5.** b.   **6.** b.   **7.** a.

~~~~~~~~~~~~~~~~~
~~~~~~~~~~~~~~~~~

Chapter Ten: MODALS, Part 2

EXERCISE 1, p. 174. *Preview.*

2. B.   **3.** A.   **4.** B.   **5.** C.   **6.** B.   **7.** A   **8.** B.   **9.** C.
10. A.   **11.** B.   **12.** B.   **13.** B.   **14.** C.

EXERCISE 4, p. 177. *Degrees of certainty: present time.*

Expected completions: **2.** must be rich.   **3.** must be crazy.   **4.** may / might / could be at a meeting   **5.** must have the wrong number.   **6.** must be

very proud.   **7.** must feel terrible.   **8.** may / might / could fit Jimmy.
9. must miss them very much.   **10.** must be about ten.

EXERCISE 5, p. 179. *Degrees of certainty: present time negative.*
   Possible responses: **2.** be at home   **3.** be thirsty   **4.** like nuts
   5. have many friends

EXERCISE 11, p. 183. *Degrees of certainty.*
   2. must not like   **3.** must have been   **4.** must be   **5.** must have
   forgotten   **6.** must not speak   **7.** must have left   **8.** must be
   9. must have hurt   **10.** must mean   **11.** must have been   **12.** must have
   misunderstood

EXERCISE 12, p. 185. *Degrees of certainty.*
   3. must   **4.** should / ought to [*also possible:* will]   **5.** should   **6.** will
   7. should / ought to   **8.** will   **9.** must   **10.** should / ought to / will
   11. should / ought to   **12.** should / ought to   **13.** should / ought to
   14. must   **15.** should have / ought to have   **16.** must have

EXERCISE 13, p. 186. *Degrees of certainty.*
   2. a. Jane   **3.** a. a rat   **4.** a. Mark   **5.** a. Janet
       b. Ron   b. a cat   b. my nieghbor   b. Sally
       c. Sue   c. a mouse   c. Carol   c. Bob
       d. Ann   d. Andy

EXERCISE 15, p. 189. *Progressive forms of modals.*
   3. must be burning   **4.** may / might / could be talking . . . may / might / could
   be talking   **5.** must be playing   **6.** may / might / could be staying . . . may /
   might / could be staying   **7.** should be studying   **8.** must be kidding
   9. may / might / could have been kidding   **10.** must have been kidding

EXERCISE 17, p. 190. *Progressive and past forms of modals.*
   2. must be waiting   **3.** shouldn't have left   **4.** might have borrowed
   5. must have been watching . . . must have forgotten   **6.** may have been attending
   [*also possible:* may have attended]   **7.** might have been washing   **8.** must
   have left   **9.** might be traveling   **10.** must not have been expecting
   11. must have been daydreaming . . . should have been paying . . . shouldn't have
   been staring   **12.** A: should have taken   B: must be walking   A: might have
   decided . . . could be working . . . may have called

EXERCISE 24, p. 195. *Using* WOULD *and* USED TO.

2. would give **3.** used to be **4.** used to be . . . would start **5.** used to be . . . would get . . . would spend . . . would find . . . would gather **6.** used to ask . . . would never let **7.** would make . . . would put **8.** would wake . . . would hike . . . would see **9.** used to take **10.** would be sitting . . . would always smile . . . would stand . . . (would) clear

EXERCISE 29, p. 202. *Review: modals and similar expressions.*

1. had better shut (should / ought to / have to / must shut)
2. could / would you hand (can / will you hand)
3. don't / won't have to go
4. can already say (is already able to say)
5. must / have to attend
6. had to wait
7. could / might go
8. would rather go
9. must not have seen
10. had better clean (should / ought to / must / have to clean)
11. can't / couldn't be (must not be) . . . may / might / could belong (must belong)
12. cannot go (must not /may not go)
13. should not have laughed
14. May / Can / Could I speak . . . can't come . . . May / Can I take
15. should / ought to take (could take) . . . can get
16. had to study . . . should have come
17. had better answer (should / ought to / have to answer) . . . might / could / may be
18. should have been / was supposed to be
19. could / might / may be
20. must have been daydreaming

EXERCISE 30, p. 204. *Error analysis: modals.*

1. If you have a car, you can <u>travel</u> around the United <u>States</u>. **2.** During class, the students must t̶o̶ sit <u>quietly</u>. When the <u>students</u> have questions, they must t̶o̶ raise their hands. **3.** When you send for the brochure, you should <u>include</u> a self-addressed, stamped envelope. **4.** A film director must <u>have</u> control over every aspect of a movie. **5.** When I was a child, I c̶a̶n̶ <u>could</u> / <u>would go</u> to the roof of my house and <u>see</u> all the other houses and streets. **6.** <u>When</u> I w̶a̶s̶ <u>worked</u> in the fields, my son would <u>bring</u> me oranes or candy. **7.** I <u>broke</u> my leg in a soccer game three <u>months</u> ago. **8.** <u>Will</u> / <u>Would</u> / <u>Could</u> you please help me with this? **9.** Many <u>students</u> would rather t̶o̶ study on their own than <u>go</u> to <u>class</u>. **10.** We <u>are</u>

supposed to bring our books to class every day.   **11.** You can <u>have</u> a very good time as a tourist in my country. My country <u>has</u> many <u>different weather areas</u>, [*also possible:* different climates] so you <u>had</u> better plan ahead before you <u>come</u>.

12. When you visit big <u>cities</u> in my country, you must ~~to be~~ <u>pay</u> attention to your wallet when you are in a <u>crowded</u> place because there <u>are</u> a lot of <u>thieves</u>.

EXERCISE 33, p. 206. *Review of verb forms.*

1. had   **2.** happened   **3.** was driving   **4.** broke   **5.** did you do

6. pulled   **7.** got   **8.** started   **9.** should not have done   **10.** should have stayed   **11.** are probably   **12.** started   **13.** have been walking / had walked   **14.** went   **15.** discovered   **16.** didn't have   **17.** can think

18. could / might have gone   **19.** could / might have tried   **20.** could / might have asked   **21.** asked   **22.** told   **23.** was   **24.** allowed

25. drove   **26.** must have felt   **27.** took   **28.** took   **29.** might get / might have gotten   **30.** will know   **31.** must / have to / should leave

32. have to / must be   **33.** May / Could / Can I use   **34.** need   **35.** don't have   **36.** will / can take

~~~~~~~~~~~~~~~~~
~~~~~~~~~~~~~~~~~

Chapter Eleven: THE PASSIVE

EXERCISE 1, p. 209. *Forming the passive.*

2. is being opened   **3.** has been opened   **4.** was opened   **5.** was being opened   **6.** had been opened   **7.** will be opened   **8.** is going to be opened   **9.** will have been opened   **10.** Is . . . being opened   **11.** Was . . . opened   **12.** Has . . . been opened

EXERCISE 2, p. 209. *Forming the passive.*

PART I.   **2.** Customers <u>are served</u> by waitresses and waiters.   **3.** The lesson <u>is going to be explained</u> by the teacher.   **4.** A new idea <u>has been suggested</u> by Shirley.

5. Ann <u>will be invited</u> to the party by Bill.   **6.** That report <u>is being prepared</u> by

Alex.   **7.** The farmer's wagon <u>was being pulled</u> by two horses.   **8.** The book <u>had been returned</u> to the library by Kathy.   **9.** By this time tomorrow, the announcement <u>will have been made</u> by the president.   **10.** That note <u>wasn't written</u> by me. It <u>was written</u> by Jim.   **11.** That pie <u>wasn't made</u> by Alice. <u>Was</u> it <u>made</u> by Mrs. French?   **12.** <u>Is</u> that course <u>taught</u> by Prof. Jackson? I know that it <u>isn't taught</u> by Prof. Adams.   **13.** Those papers <u>haven't been signed</u> by Mrs. Andrews yet. <u>Have</u> they <u>been signed</u> by Mr. Andrews?   **14.** <u>Is</u> your house <u>being painted</u> by Mr. Brown?   **15.** I <u>won't be fooled</u> by his tricks.

PART II.   **16.** Omar <u>wrote</u> that sentence.   **17.** The teacher <u>is going to collect</u> our papers.   **18.** <u>Did</u> Thomas Edison <u>invent</u> the electric light bulb?
19. Most drivers <u>don't obey</u> the speed limit on Highway 5.   **20.** <u>Has</u> the building superintendent <u>informed</u> you of a proposed increase in our rent?

EXERCISE 3, p. 210. *Forming the passive.*

3. *(no change)*   **4.** *(no change)*   **5.** That theory was developed by Dr. Ikeda.
6. The cup was dropped by Timmy.   **7.** *(no change)*   **8.** I was interviewed by the assistant manager.   **9.** *(no change)*   **10.** The small fishing village was destroyed by a hurricane.   **11.** *(no change)*   **12.** *(no change)*
13. *(no change)*   **14.** After class, the chalkboard is always erased by one of the students.   **15.** *(no change)*   **16.** *(no change)*   **17.** *(no change)*
18. The fire wasn't caused by lightning.   **19.** The dispute is going to be settled by a special committee.   **20.** Was the enemy surrounded by the army?
21. *(no change)*   **22.** Windmills were invented by the Persians around 1500 years ago.

EXERCISE 5, p. 212. *Using the passive.*

3. This antique table was made in 1734.   **4.** *(no change)*   **5.** My purse was stolen.   **6.** The coffee was being made when I walked into the kitchen.
7. That book has been translated into many languages.   **8.** That picture was drawn by Jim's daughter. This picture was drawn by my son.   **9.** The applicants will be judged on the basis of their originality.   **10.** *(no change)*   **11.** Is that course being taught by Professor Rivers this semester?   **12.** When was the radio invented?   **13.** The mail had already been delivered by the time I left for school this morning.   **14.** When are the results of the contest going to be announced?
15. After the concert was over, the rock music star was mobbed by hundreds of fans outside the theater.   **16.** Ever since I arrived here, I have been living in the dormitory because I was told that it was cheaper to live there than in an apartment.

17. The new hospital is going to be built next year. The new elementary school has already been built.   **18.** If a film is exposed to light while it is being developed, the negative will be ruined.

EXERCISE 6, p. 213. *Indirect objects as passive subjects.*

2. Peggy = indirect object — Peggy was awarded a scholarship by Indiana University.

3. Fred = indirect object — Fred was paid three hundred dollars in consulting fees.

4. Maria = indirect object — Maria was given a promotion at her job as a computer programmer at Microsoft.

5. you = indirect object — You will be sent a bill.

6. people = indirect object — The starving people will be given a week's supply of rice.

EXERCISE 7, p. 213. *Using the passive.*

1. You were invited to a party.   **2.** Rice is grown in many countries.   **3.** The game is being televised.   **4.** Reading is taught in the first grade.   **5.** You were told to be here at ten.   **6.** That hat was made in Mexico.   **7.** Dinner is going to be served at six.   **8.** The news will be announced tomorrow.   **9.** A mistake has been made.

10. A test is being given (by the teacher) in the next room right now.

EXERCISE 9, p. 215. *Using the passive.*

2. is surrounded   **3.** is spelled   **4.** will be built / is going to be built

5. was divided / has been divided   **6.** is worn   **7.** was caused

8. was ordered   **9.** who was accidentally killed   **10.** was reported

11. was surprised / hadn't expected   **12.** was offered   **13.** were frightened

14. was confused   **15.** is expected / is reported

EXERCISE 10, p. 216. *Using the passive.*

1. is produced   **2.** is being treated   **3.** will probably be won   **4.** saw . . . was interviewed   **5.** are controlled / are determined   **6.** was caught . . . was being chased . . . jumped . . . kept   **7.** appeared . . . have been named . . . described . . . are being discovered / are discovered   **8.** was informed . . . was told   **9.** is exposed . . . affects   **10.** was discovered . . . called . . . was translated . . . had been built . . . do not exist   **11.** was recognized . . . was asked . . . took . . . knew . . . multiplied . . . came   **12.** brought . . . sent . . . were asked . . . was discovered . . . is still called

EXERCISE 11, p. 219. *Passive modals.*

4. must be kept   5. must keep   6. couldn't be opened   7. couldn't open
8. may be offered   9. may offer   10. may already have been offered /
may have already been offered   11. may already have offered / may have already
offered   12. ought to be divided   13. ought to have been divided   14. have to
be returned   15. has to return . . . will have to pay   16. had better be
finished   17. had better finish   18. is supposed to be sent   19. should have
been sent   20. must have been surprised

EXERCISE 12, p. 220. *Passive modals.*

Expected completions: 2. must be married   3. must be written / have to be
written   4. must have been left   5. should / ought to / has to be postponed
6. should not be given   7. should / ought to be encouraged   8. may / could /
might / will be misunderstood   9. cannot be explained   10. must have been
embarrassed   11. must / has to be pushed   12. should / ought to have been
built   13. must / should be saved   14. must / has to / should be done
15. ought to / should be elected

EXERCISE 14, p. 222. *Using the passive.*

1. is usually delivered [*also possible:* usually gets delivered]   2. were working . . .
occurred . . . was hurt [*also possible:* was hurt]   3. was not admitted . . . had
already begun   4. had already been offered   5. is being organized   6. will
never be forgotten / is never going to be forgotten   7. was . . . happened . . .
flunked . . . dropped . . . was walking . . . fell . . . was stolen [*also possible:* got stolen]
8. had already been rented   9. was being ignored   10. did you buy . . . didn't
buy . . . was given . . . Do you like   11. is circled . . . are held . . . are circled
12. worshipped   13. have been destroyed   14. were allowed . . . were not
invited . . . were forbidden . . . were being held / were held   15. was built . . . has
often been described . . . was designed . . . took   16. is being judged . . . will be
announced / are going to be announced

EXERCISE 16, p. 224. *Using the passive.*

1. paper has been made from various plants . . . In the past, paper was made by hand
. . . Today paper is made from wood pulp   2. In the mechanical process, wood is
ground . . . During the grinding, it is sprayed . . . Then the chips are soaked
3. First the wood is washed and then it is cut into small pieces . . . Then the chips are
cooked . . . After the wood is cooked, it is washed   4. The pulp is drained to
form . . . (is) bleached . . . and then (is) thoroughly washed again. Next the pulp is
put . . . drier and a press, they are wound   5. . . . how it is made.

EXERCISE 18, p. 226. *Stative passive.*

2. is shut   **3.** are turned   **4.** is not crowded   **5.** are bent . . . are folded
6. is finished   **7.** is closed   **8.** was closed   **9.** is stuck   **10.** was stuck
11. is made . . . (is) swept . . . (are) washed   **12.** is set . . . (are) done . . . (are)
lighted / (are) lit   **13.** is gone   **14.** is torn   **15.** is hidden

EXERCISE 19, p. 226. *Stative passive.*

2. is . . . crowded   **3.** is scheduled   **4.** am exhausted   **5.** am confused
6. is stuck   **7.** are turned off   **8.** is insured   **9.** are divorced
10. is gone   **11.** are . . . qualified   **12.** am married   **13.** is spoiled
14. is blocked   **15.** is located   **16.** was born   **17.** is . . . turned off
18. are . . . done

EXERCISE 20, p. 228. *Stative passive + prepositions.*

2. with   **3.** for   **4.** to   **5.** to   **6.** with   **7.** in   **8.** with
9. to   **10.** to   **11.** with   **12.** of   **13.** to   **14.** to . . . of
15. with   **16.** from   **17.** with   **18.** in   **19.** to   **20.** with
21. to   **22.** with   **23.** for   **24.** in/with . . . to . . . with
25. with . . . in . . . to

EXERCISE 22, p. 230. *Stative passive + prepositions.*

2. is composed of   **3.** am accustomed to   **4.** is terrified of   **5.** is finished
with   **6.** is addicted to   **7.** is covered with   **8.** am satisfied with
9. is married to   **10.** is divorced from   **11.** am . . . acquainted with
12. am tired of   **13.** Are . . . related to   **14.** is dedicated to   **15.** is
disappointed in   **16.** is scared of   **17.** is committed to   **18.** are devoted to
19. is dressed in   **20.** are done with

EXERCISE 23, p. 232. *The passive with* GET.

2. am getting sleepy   **3.** is getting late   **4.** got wet   **5.** is getting hot
6. get nervous   **7.** is getting dark   **8.** got light   **9.** am getting full
10. is getting better   **11.** Get busy   **12.** Get well

EXERCISE 24, p. 233. *The passive with* GET.

2. got hurt   **3.** got lost   **4.** get dressed   **5.** did . . . get married / are . . .
getting / going to get married   **6.** get accustomed   **7.** am getting worried
8. get upset   **9.** got confused   **10.** get done   **11.** got depressed
12. Did . . . get invited   **13.** got bored   **14.** get packed   **15.** get paid

16. got hired   **17.** got fired   **18.** didn't get finished   **19.** got disgusted
20. got engaged . . . got married . . . got divorced . . . got remarried

EXERCISE 26, p. 235. *Participial adjectives.*
  3. exciting   **4.** excited   **5.** surprising   **6.** surprised   **7.** frightened
  8. frightening   **9.** exhausting   **10.** exhausted

EXERCISE 28, p. 236. *Participial adjectives.*
  2. satisfying   **3.** terrifying   **4.** terrified   **5.** embarrassing
  6. broken   **7.** crowded   **8.** locked   **9.** injured   **10.** annoying
  11. challenging   **12.** expected   **13.** growing . . . balanced   **14.** spoiled
  15. sleeping   **16.** thrilling   **17.** abandoned   **18.** required
  19. Polluted   **20.** furnished   **21.** dividing   **22.** elected
  23. printing   **24.** Experienced   **25.** amazing

EXERCISE 29, p. 237. *Error analysis: the passive.*
  2. Two people got <u>hurt</u> in the accident and were <u>taken</u> to the hospital by an ambulance.   **3.** The movie was so <u>boring</u> that we fell asleep after an hour.
4. The students <u>were</u> helped by the clear explanation that the teacher gave.
5. That alloy is <u>composed of</u> iron and tin.   **6.** The winner of the race hasn't been <u>announced</u> yet.   **7.** If you are <u>interested</u> in modern art, you should see the new exhibit at the museum. It is <u>fascinating</u>.   **8.** Progress is <u>being</u> made every day.
9. When and where <u>was</u> the automobile invented?   **10.** My brother and I have always been <u>interested</u> in learning more about our family tree.   **11.** I <u>don't</u> agree with you, and I don't think you'll ever ~~to~~ convince me.   **12.** Each assembly kit is <u>accompanied</u> by detailed instructions.   **13.** Arthur was <u>given</u> an award by the city for all of his efforts in crime prevention.   **14.** It was late, and I was getting very <u>worried</u> about my mother.   **15.** The problem was very <u>puzzling</u>. I couldn't figure it out.   **16.** Many strange things ~~were~~ happened last night.   **17.** How many <u>people</u> have you ~~been~~ invited to the party?   OR   How many <u>people</u> have ~~you~~ been invited to the party?   **18.** When I returned home, everything <u>was quiet</u>. I <u>walked</u> to my room, <u>got undressed</u>, and <u>went</u> to bed.   **19.** I didn't go to dinner with them because I had already ~~been~~ eaten.   **20.** In class yesterday, I was <u>confused</u>. I didn't understand the lesson.   **21.** I couldn't move. I was very <u>frightened</u>.
22. When we were children, we <u>were</u> very afraid of caterpillars. Whenever we saw one of these monsters, we <u>ran</u> / <u>would</u> run to our house before the caterpillars could attack us. I am still <u>scared</u> when I <u>see</u> a caterpillar close to me.   **23.** One day, while the old man was cutting down a big tree near the stream, his axe <u>fell</u> into the

river. He sat down and <u>began</u> to cry because he <u>did</u> not have enough money to buy another axe.

~~~~~~~~~~~~~~~~

~~~~~~~~~~~~~~~~

Chapter Twelve: NOUN CLAUSES

EXERCISE 1, p. 240. *Noun clauses.*

3. Where did Tom go? **N**o one knows.   4. No one knows <u>where Tom went</u>.
5. <u>Where Tom went</u> is a secret.   6. What does Anna want? **W**e need to know.
7. We need to know <u>what Anna wants</u>.   8. What does Alex need? **D**o you know?
9. Do you know <u>what Alex needs</u>?   10. <u>What Alex needs</u> is a new job.
11. We talked about <u>what Alex needs</u>.   12. What do you need? **D**id you talk to your parents about <u>what you need</u>?

EXERCISE 2, p. 241. *Noun clauses beginning with a question word.*

3. where you live   4. What she said   5. when they are coming   6. how much it costs   7. which one he wants   8. who is coming to the party   9. who those people are   10. whose pen this is   11. Why they left the country
12. What we are doing in class   13. Where she went   14. how many letters there are in the English alphabet   15. who the mayor of New York City is
16. how old a person has to be to get a driver's license   17. what happened
18. who opened the door

EXERCISE 3, p. 242. *Noun clauses beginning with a question word.*

I don't know . . . .
1. where (. . .) lives.   2. what country (. . .) is from.   3. how long (. . .) has been living here.   4. what (. . .)'s telephone number is.   5. where the post office is.   6. how far it is to (Kansas City).   7. why (. . .) is absent.
8. where my book is.   9. what kind of watch (. . .) has.   10. why (. . .) was absent yesterday.   11. where (. . .) went yesterday.   12. what kind of

government (Italy) has.   **13.** what (. . .)'s favorite color is.   **14.** how long (. . .) has been married.   **15.** why we are doing this exercise.   **16.** who turned off the lights.   **17.** where (. . .) is going to eat lunch/dinner. **18.** when (the semester) ends.   **19.** where (. . .) went after class yesterday. **20.** why (. . .) is smiling.   **21.** how often (. . .) goes to the library. **22.** whose book that is.   **23.** how much that book cost.   **24.** who took my book.

EXERCISE 4, p. 242. *Noun clauses beginning with a question word.*

2. Why is he coming? Please tell me why he is coming.   **3.** Which flight will he be on? Please tell me which flight he will be on.   **4.** Who is going to meet him at the airport? Please tell me who is going to meet him at the airport.   **5.** Who is his roommate? Please tell me who his roommate is.   **6.** What is Tom's address? Please tell me what Tom's address is.   **7.** Where does he live? Please tell me where he lives.   **8.** Where was he last week? Please tell me where he was last week. **9.** How long has he been working for IBM? Do you know how long he has been working for IBM?   **10.** What kind of computer does he have at home? Do you know what kind of computer he has at home?

EXERCISE 5, p. 243. *Noun clauses beginning with a question word.*

2. is my eraser . . . it is   **3.** didn't Fred lock . . . he didn't lock   **4.** has he been . . . he has lived   **5.** you are taking . . . are you taking   **6.** are we supposed . . . we are supposed

EXERCISE 7, p. 246. *Noun clauses beginning with* WHETHER *or* IF.

I wonder . . . .

1. where my friend is.   **2.** whether/if we should wait for him.   **3.** whether/if I should call him.   **4.** where my dictionary is.   **5.** who took my dictionary. **6.** whether/if (. . .) borrowed my dictionary.   **7.** who that woman is. **8.** whether/if she needs any help.   **9.** why the sky is blue.   **10.** how long a butterfly lives.   **11.** what causes earthquakes.   **12.** when the first book was written.   **13.** who that man is.   **14.** what he is doing.   **15.** whether/if he is having trouble.   **16.** whether/if I should offer to help him.   **17.** how far it is to (Florida).   **18.** whether/if we have enough time to go to (Florida) over vacation.   **19.** whose book this is.   **20.** whether/if it belongs to (. . .). / who it belongs to.   **21.** why dinosaurs became extinct.   **22.** whether/if there is life on other planets.   **23.** how life began.   **24.** whether/if people will live on the moon someday.

EXERCISE 8, p. 246. *Noun clauses.*

Could you please tell me . . . .

1. if this bus goes downtown?   **2.** how much this book costs?   **3.** when Flight 62 is expected to arrive?   **4.** where the nearest phone is?   **5.** whether/if this word is spelled correctly?   **6.** what time it is?   **7.** if this information is correct?   **8.** how much it costs to fly from (Chicago) to (New York)?   **9.** where the bus station is?   **10.** whose pen this is?

EXERCISE 9, p. 247. *Error analysis: noun clauses.*

2. No one seems to know when <u>Maria will arrive</u>.   **3.** I wonder why <u>Bob was late</u> for class.   **4.** I don't know what ~~does~~ that word <u>means</u>.   **5.** I wonder ~~does~~ <u>whether/if</u> the teacher <u>knows</u> the answer.   **6.** What <u>they should</u> do about the hole in their roof is their most pressing problem.   **7.** I'll ask her <u>whether/if she would like</u> some coffee or not.   **8.** Be sure to tell the doctor where ~~does~~ it <u>hurts</u>. **9.** Why <u>I am</u> unhappy is something I can't explain.   **10.** I wonder ~~does~~ <u>whether/if</u> Tom <u>knows</u> about the meeting or not.   **11.** I need to know who <u>your teacher is</u>. **12.** I don't understand why <u>the car is not running</u> properly.   **13.** My young son wants to know where ~~do~~ the stars go in the daytime.

EXERCISE 10, p. 247. *Question words followed by infinitives.*

2. The plumber told me how <u>to fix</u> the leak in the sink.   **3.** Please tell me where <u>to meet</u> you.   **4.** . . . Sandy didn't know whether <u>to believe</u> him or not. **5.** . . . deciding which one <u>to buy</u>.   **6.** . . . I don't know what else <u>to do</u>. *Possible completions:*   **7.** to say   **8.** what to wear   **9.** to live in a dormitory or an apartment   **10.** to ski   **11.** to give (. . .)   **12.** to accept the job offer or (to) stay in graduate school   **13.** to go . . . to get there

EXERCISE 11, p. 249. *Noun clauses beginning with* THAT.

Possible sentences: **1.** It is a pity that Tim hasn't been able to make any friends. That Tim hasn't been able to make any friends is a pity.   **2.** It is a well-known fact that drug abuse can ruin one's health. That drug abuse can ruin one's health is a well-known fact.   **3.** It is unfair that some women do not earn equal pay for equal work. That some women do not earn equal pay for equal work is unfair. **4.** It is true that the earth revolves around the sun. That the earth revolves around the sun is true.   **5.** It is surprising that Irene, who is an excellent student, failed her entrance examination. That Irene, who is an excellent student, failed her entrance examination is surprising.   **6.** It is apparent that smoking can cause cancer. That smoking can cause cancer is apparent.   **7.** It is a fact that English is the principal language of the business community throughout much of the world. That English is the principal language of the business community throughout much of the world is a fact.

EXERCISE 12, p. 249. *Noun clauses beginning with* THAT.
Sample responses: **1.** It is a fact that the world is round. That the world is round is a fact. **2.** It is surprising that vegetation can survive in a desert. That vegetation can survive in a desert is surprising. **3.** It is obvious that you need to wear warm clothing when it's cold. That you need to wear warm clothing when it's cold is obvious. **4.** It is too bad that prejudice influences so many people. That prejudice influences so many people is too bad. **5.** It is a well-known fact that two plus two equals four. That two plus two equals four is a well-known fact. **6.** It is unfortunate that we don't all speak the same language. That we don't all speak the same language is unfortunate. **7.** It is true that cities are noisy. That cities are noisy is true. **8.** It is strange that we are destroying our own natural resources. That we are destroying our own natural resources is strange. **9.** It is unlikely that you will live to be one hundred. That you will live to be one hundred is unlikely. **10.** It is undeniable that the sun rises in the east. That the sun rises in the east is undeniable.

EXERCISE 13, p. 249. *Noun clauses beginning with* THAT.
Sample completions: **2.** It seems to me that winters are becoming milder. **3.** It is my impression that time seems to go faster as I grow older. **4.** It is my theory that young drivers are more reckless than older drivers. **5.** It is widely believed that herbs can heal. **6.** It is thought that you can't teach an old dog new tricks. **7.** It has been said that children are more influenced by their peers than by their parents. **8.** It is a miracle that more people aren't killed in automobile accidents.

EXERCISE 14, p. 250. *Noun clauses beginning with* THAT.
Sample completions: **2.** . . . we had this time together. **3.** . . . I wasn't able to get a ticket to the soccer finals. **4.** . . . you have been my teacher this year. **5.** . . . (Yoko) quit school. **6.** . . . you will like this restaurant as much as we do. **7.** . . . the prices are so reasonable. **8.** . . . it isn't raining today. **9.** . . . my bus was late. **10.** . . . I'm going to be late in paying the money I owe you.

EXERCISE 15, p. 250. *Noun clauses beginning with* THAT.
Sample completions: **3.** One reason is that I want to study at an American university. Another reason is that I need to pass a written driver's test. A third is that I need to find a good part-time job. **4.** One problem is that I'm homesick. Another problem is that I can't understand people when they speak fast. A third

problem I have had is that I am having trouble finding an apartment for my family.
5. One advantage of owning your own car is that you don't need to rely on public transportation. Another advantage is that you can travel into the country on weekends. One disadvantage, however, of owning your own car is that it is expensive.

EXERCISE 16, p. 250. *Noun clauses beginning with* THAT.
2. The fact that Rosa didn't come made me angry.   **3.** I feel fine except for the fact that I'm a little tired.   **4.** Natasha was not admitted to the university due to the fact that she didn't pass the entrance examination.   **5.** The fact that many people in the world live in intolerable poverty must concern us all.   **6.** The fact that Surasuk is frequently absent from class indicates his lack of interest in school.   **7.** I was not aware of the fact that I was supposed to bring my passport to the examination for identification.   **8.** Due to the fact that the people of the town were given no warning of the approaching tornado, there were many casualties.

EXERCISE 17, p. 252. *Quoted speech.*
   1. Henry said, "There is a phone call for you."
   2. "There is a phone call for you," he said.
   3. "There is," said Henry, "a phone call for you."
   4. "There is a phone call for you. It's your sister," said Henry.
   5. "There is a phone call for you," he said. "It's your sister."
   6. I asked him, "Where is the phone?"
   7. "Where is the phone?" she asked.
   8. "Stop the clock!" shouted the referee. "We have an injured player."
   9. "Who won the game?" asked the spectator.
  10.   "I'm going to rest for the next three hours," she said. "I don't want to be disturbed."
         "That's fine," I replied. "You get some rest. I'll make sure no one disturbs you."

EXERCISE 18, p. 252. *Quoted speech.*
      When the police officer came over to my car, he said, "Let me see your driver's license, please."
      "What's wrong, Officer?" I asked. "Was I speeding?"
      "No, you weren't speeding," he replied. "You went through a red light at the corner of Fifth Avenue and Main Street. You almost caused an accident."
      "Did I really do that?" I said. "I didn't see a red light."

EXERCISE 21, p. 254. *Reported speech.*

4. if I was hungry. **5.** (that) she wanted a sandwich. **6.** (that) he was going to move to Ohio. **7.** whether/if I had enjoyed my trip. **8.** what I was talking about. **9.** whether/if I had seen her grammar book. **10.** (that) she didn't want to go. **11.** where Nadia was. **12.** Whether/If I could help him with his report. **13.** (that) he might be late. **14.** (that) I should work harder. **15.** (that) she had to go downtown. **16.** why the sky is blue. **17.** why I was tired. **18.** (that) he would come to the meeting. **19.** whether/if Ms. Chang would be in class tomorrow / the next day. **20.** that the sun rises in the east. **21.** (that) someday we would be in contact with beings from outer space. **22.** (that) he thought he would go to the library to study. **23.** whether/if Omar knew what he was doing. **24.** whether/if what I had heard was true. **25.** that sentences with noun clauses are a little complicated.

EXERCISE 24, p. 257. *Reported speech: verb forms in noun clauses.*

3. was going . . . didn't know . . . worked **4.** where the chess match would take . . . hadn't been decided **5.** was . . . didn't think . . . would . . . speak . . . was getting . . . would be speaking **6.** were . . . might be . . . could develop

EXERCISE 25, p. 258. *Reported speech.*

2. she was excited about her new job and (that she) had found a nice apartment. **3.** my Uncle Harry was in the hospital and that Aunt Sally was very worried about him. **4.** that s/he expected us to be in class every day and that unexcused absences might affect our grades. **5.** that Highway 66 would be closed for two months and that commuters should seek alternate routes. **6.** that he was getting good grades but (that he) had difficulty understanding lectures. **7.** that every obstacle was a steppingstone to success and that I should view problems in my life as opportunities to prove myself. **8.** that she would come to the meeting but (that she) couldn't stay for more than an hour.

EXERCISE 30, p. 261. *Error analysis: noun clauses.*

1. Tell the taxi driver where ~~do~~ you want to go. **2.** My roommate came into the room and asked me why I wasn't in class. I told him / said (that) I was waiting for a telephone call from my family. OR My roommate came into the room and asked ~~me~~, "Why aren't you in class?" I said, "I am waiting for a telephone call from my family." **3.** It was my first day at the university, and I was on my way to my first class. I wondered who else would be in the class and what the teacher would be like. **4.** He asked me what ~~did~~ I intended to do after I graduated. **5.** Many of the people in the United States do not know much about geography. For example,

46

people will ask you where <u>Japan is located</u>.   **6.** What <s>does</s> a patient <u>tells</u> a doctor <s>it</s> is confidential.   **7.** What my friend and I did <s>it</s> was our secret. We didn't even tell our parents <u>what we did</u>.   **8.** The doctor asked <u>whether/if</u> I felt okay. I told him that I <u>didn't</u> feel well.   **9.** <u>It is</u> clear that the ability to use a computer <s>it</s> is an important skill in the modern world.   **10.** I asked him, "What kind of movies <u>do you like</u>? **H**e said <s>me</s>, "I like romantic movies."   OR   I asked him what kind of movies <u>he liked</u>. **H**e <u>told</u> me / said <u>(that) he liked</u> romantic movies.   **11.** "<u>Is it</u> true you almost drowned?" my friend asked me. "Yes," I said. "I'm really glad to be alive. It was really frightening."   **12.** <u>The fact that</u> I almost drowned makes me very careful about water safety whenever I go swimming.   **13.** I didn't know where I <u>was</u> supposed to get off the bus, so I asked the driver where <u>the science museum was</u>. She <u>told</u> me the name of the street. She said she <u>would</u> tell me when I <u>should</u> get off the bus.   **14.** My mother did not live with us. When other children asked me where <s>was</s> <u>my mother was</u>, I told them she <u>was</u> going to come to visit me very soon.   **15.** When I asked the taxi driver to drive faster, he said, "I will drive faster if you pay me more."   OR   he said he would drive faster if I paid him more. At that time I didn't care how much <u>it would</u> cost, so I told him to go as fast as he <u>could</u>.   **16.** We looked back to see where <u>we were</u> and how far <u>we were</u> from camp. We <u>didn't</u> know, so we decided to turn back. We <u>were</u> afraid that we <u>had wandered</u> too far.   **17.** After the accident, I opened my eyes slowly and <u>realized</u> that I <u>was</u> still alive.   **18.** My country is prospering due to <s>it is a</s> <u>the fact</u> that it has become a leading producer of oil.   **19.** <u>It is</u> true that one must know <u>English</u> in order to study at an <u>American</u> university.   **20.** My mother told me <s>what it was</s> the purpose of our visit.   OR   what <s>it</s> <u>the purpose of our visit was</u>.

EXERCISE 35, p. 264. *Using the subjunctive in noun clauses.*
   Possible completions: **2.** call   **3.** tell   **4.** speak   **5.** write
   6. see   **7.** contact   **8.** be

EXERCISE 36, p. 264. *Using the subjunctive in noun clauses.*
   1. take   **2.** be named   **3.** stay   **4.** be postponed   **5.** be admitted
   6. be controlled . . . (be) eliminated   **7.** have   **8.** be   **9.** know
   10. be   **11.** be permitted   **12.** not be   **13.** return   **14.** be built
   15. not tell . . . be told

EXERCISE 37, p. 265. *Using -EVER words.*
   2. whenever   **3.** whatever   **4.** whichever   **5.** whatever   **6.** Whoever
   7. whatever   **8.** however   **9.** whoever   **10.** wherever   **11.** whomever / whoever . . . whomever / whoever   **12.** whatever   **13.** whichever

14. wherever   **15.** whatever . . . wherever . . . whenever . . . whomever / whoever
. . . however

~~~~~~~~~~~~~~~~~~
~~~~~~~~~~~~~~~~~~

Chapter Thirteen: ADJECTIVE CLAUSES

EXERCISE 1, p. 268. *Adjective clause pronouns used as subjects.*
Note: The adjective clauses are underlined.
2. The girl who/that won the race is happy.   **3.** The student who/that sits next to
me is from China.   **4.** The students who/that sit in the front row are from China.
5. We are studying sentences which/that contain adjective clauses.   **6.** I am using
a sentence which/that contains an adjective clause.   **7.** Algebra problems contain
letters which/that stand for unknown numbers.   **8.** The taxi driver who/that took
me to the airport was friendly.

EXERCISE 2, p. 269. *Adjective clause pronouns used as the object of a verb.*
Note: The adjective clauses are underlined.
1. The book which/that Ø I read was good.   **2.** I liked the woman who(m)/that/Ø
I met at the party last night.   **3.** I liked the composition which/that/Ø you wrote.
4. The people who(m)/that/Ø we visited yesterday were very nice.   **5.** The man
who(m)/that/Ø I was telling you about is standing over there.   OR   about whom I was
telling you is standing over there.

EXERCISE 3, p. 269. *Adjective clause pronouns used the object of a preposition.*
Note: The adjective clauses are underlined.
1. The meeting which/that/Ø I went to was interesting.   OR   The meeting to which
I went was interesting.   **2.** The man to whom I talked yesterday was very kind.   OR
The man who(m)/that/Ø I talked to yesterday was very kind.   **3.** I must thank the
people from whom I got a present.   OR   I must thank the people who(m)/that/Ø I got
a present from.   **4.** The picture which/that/Ø she was looking at was beautiful.
OR   The picture at which she was looking was beautiful.   **5.** The man about whom I

was telling you is over there.   OR   The man who(m)/that/Ø I was telling you about is over there.   **6.** I ran into a woman with whom I had gone to elementary school. OR   I ran into a woman who(m)/that/Ø I had gone to elementary school with. **7.** The topic about which Omar talked was interesting.   OR   The topic which/that/ Ø Omar talked about was interesting.   **8.** The people to/with whom I spoke were friendly.   OR   The people who(m)/that/Ø I spoke to/with were friendly.   **9.** Olga wrote on a topic about which she knew nothing.   OR   Olga wrote on a topic which/that/Ø she knew nothing about.   **10.** The candidate for whom I voted didn't win the election.   OR   The candidate who(m)/that/Ø I voted for didn't win the election.

EXERCISE 4, p. 270. *Adjective clauses.*

Note: The adjective clauses are underlined.

1. I met last night — Did I tell you about the woman who(m)/that I met last night?   **2.** I was dancing with — The woman who(m)/that I was dancing with stepped on my toe.   OR   The woman with whom I was dancing stepped on my toe. **3.** Joe is writing — The report which/that Joe is writing must be finished by Friday.   **4.** who examined the sick child — The doctor who/that examined the sick child was gentle.   **5.** I was waiting for — The people who(m)/that I was waiting for were late.   OR   The people for whom I was waiting were late.   **6.** that occurred in California — Did you hear about the earthquake which occurred in California?

EXERCISE 5, p. 270. *Adjective clauses.*

Note: The adjective clauses are underlined.

1. She lectured on a topic which/that/Ø I know very little about.   OR   She lectured on a topic about which I know very little. [*usual:* topic I know very little about]   **2.** The students who/that were absent from class missed the assignment. [*usual:* students who were absent from class]   **3.** Yesterday I ran into an old friend who(m)/that/Ø I hadn't seen for years. [*usual:* friend I hadn't seen for years] **4.** The young women who(m)/that/Ø we met at the meeting last night are all from Japan. [*usual:* women we met at the meeting last night]   **5.** I am reading a book which/that was written by Jane Austen. [*usual:* book that was written by Jane Austen]   **6.** The man who(m)/that/Ø I spoke to gave me good advice.   OR   The man to whom I spoke gave me good advice. [*usual:* man I spoke to]   **7.** I returned the money which/that/Ø I had borrowed from my roommate. [*usual:* money I had borrowed from my roommate]   **8.** The dogcatcher caught the dog which/that had bitten my neighbor's daughter. [*usual:* dog that had bitten my neighbor's daughter] **9.** I read about a man who/that keeps chickens in his apartment. [*usual:* man who keeps chickens in his apartment]

EXERCISE 6, p. 271. *Adjective clauses.*

1. In our village, there were many people <u>who</u> didn't have much money.   OR   In our village, many people didn't have much money.   2. I enjoyed the book (that) you told me to read ~~it~~.   3. I still remember the man who ~~he~~ taught me to play the violin when I was a boy.   4. I showed my father a picture of the car I am going to buy ~~it~~ as soon as I save enough money.   5. The woman about <u>whom</u> I was talking ~~about~~ suddenly walked into the room.   OR   The woman ~~about~~ <u>who(m)/that/Ø</u> I was talking about suddenly walked into the room. I hope she didn't hear me.

6. Almost all of the people <u>who/that</u> appear on television wear makeup.

7. I don't like to spend time with people <u>who/that lose</u> their temper easily.

8. The boy drew pictures of people at an airport <u>who/that were</u> waiting for their planes.   OR   The boy drew pictures of people <u>who/that were</u> waiting for their planes at an airport.   9. People who <u>work</u> in the hunger program ~~they~~ estimate that 3500 people in the world die from starvation every day of the year.   10. In one corner of the marketplace, an old man ~~who~~ was playing a violin.   OR   In one corner of the marketplace, there <u>was</u> an old man who was playing a violin.

EXERCISE 8, p. 273. *Adjective clauses.*

1. Yes, the chair I am sitting in is comfortable.   2. Yes, the man I saw was wearing a brown suit.   3. Yes, the woman I talked to answered my questions.

4. Yes, the woman who stepped on my toe apologized.   5. Yes, most of the students who took the test passed.   6. Yes, the meat I had for dinner last night was good.

7. Yes, the woman who shouted at me was angry.   8. Yes, I know the person who is sitting next to me.   9. Yes, I recognize the woman who came into the room.

10. Yes, the coat I bought keeps me warm.   11. Yes, the TV program I watched last night was good.   12. Yes, I finished the book I was reading.   13. Yes, the hotel I stayed at was in the middle of the city.   OR   Yes, the hotel where I stayed was in the middle of the city.   14. Yes, the exercise we are doing is easy.   15. Yes, the waiter who served me at the restaurant was polite.   16. Yes, the student who stopped me in the hall asked me for the correct time.   17. Yes, all the students who are sitting in this room can speak English.   18. Yes, I found the book I was looking for.   19. Yes, the boots/tennis shoes/loafers I am wearing are comfortable.

20. Yes, I had a conversation with the taxi driver who took me to the bus station.

21. Yes, I thanked the man who opened the door for me.   22. Yes, the clerk who cashed my check asked for identification.   23. Yes, the package I got in the mail was from my parents.   24. Yes, the man who stopped me on the street asked me for directions.

50

EXERCISE 10, p. 275. *Using* WHOSE *in adjective clauses.*

Note: The adjective clauses are underlined.

2. I apologized to the woman whose coffee I spilled.   **3.** The man whose wallet was stolen called the police.   **4.** I met the woman whose husband is the president of the corporation.   **5.** The professor whose course I am taking is excellent.

6. Mr. North teaches a class for students whose native language is not English.

7. The people whose house we visited were nice.   **8.** I live in a dormitory whose residents come from many countries.   **9.** I have to call the man whose umbrella I accidentally picked up after the meeting.   **10.** The man whose beard caught on fire when he lit a cigarette poured a glass of water on his face. [*Note: "when he lit a cigarette" is an adverb clause connected to an adjective clause.*]

EXERCISE 11, p. 275. *Using* WHOSE *in adjective clauses.*

Note: The adjective clauses are underlined.

1. Maria is **a** student. I found her book. Maria is **the** student whose book I found.

2. Omar is **a** student. I borrowed his dictionary. Omar is **the** student whose dictionary I borrowed.   **3.** I used a woman's phone. I thanked her. I thanked **the** woman whose phone I used.   **4.** I broke a child's toy. He started to cry. **The** child whose toy I broke started to cry.   **5.** I stayed at a family's house. They were very kind. **The** family at whose house I stayed were very kind. OR **The** family whose house I stayed at were very kind.   **6. A** woman's purse was stolen. She called the police. **The** woman whose purse was stolen called the police.   **7.** (Placido Domingo) is **a** singer. I like his music best. (Placido Domingo) is **the** singer whose music I like best.   **8.** Everyone tried to help **a** family. Their house had burned down. Everyone tried to help **the** family whose house had burned down.

EXERCISE 12, p. 276. *Using* WHOSE *in adjective clauses.*

Note: The adjective clauses are underlined.

3. There is the boy whose father is a doctor.   **4.** There is the girl whose mother is a dentist.   **5.** There is the person whose picture was in the newspaper.   **6.** There is the woman whose car was stolen.   **7.** There is the man whose daughter won a gold medal at the Olympic Games.   **8.** There is the woman whose keys I found.

9. There is the teacher whose class I'm in.   **10.** There is the man whose wife we met.   **11.** There is the author whose book I read.   **12.** There is the student whose lecture notes I borrowed.

EXERCISE 13, p. 276. *Using* WHOSE *in adjective clauses.*

Note: The adjective clauses are underlined.

3. The students whose names were called raised their hands.   **4.** Jack knows a man whose name is William Blueheart Duckbill, Jr.   **5.** The police came to question the woman whose purse was stolen outside the supermarket.   **6.** The day care center was established to take care of children whose parents work during the day.   **7.** We couldn't find the person whose car was blocking the driveway.   **8.** The professor told the three students whose reports were turned in late that he would accept the papers this time, but never again.

EXERCISE 14, p. 277. *Using* WHERE *in adjective clauses.*
Note: The adjective clauses are underlined.
1. The city where we took our vacation was beautiful.   OR   The city which/that/Ø we took our vacation in was beautiful.   OR   The city in which we took our vacation was beautiful.   **2.** That is the restaurant where I will meet you.   OR   That is the restaurant which/that/Ø I will meet you in.   OR   That is the restaurant in which I will meet you.   **3.** The town where I grew up is small.   OR   The town which/that/Ø I grew up in is small.   OR   The town in which I grew up is small.
4. That is the drawer where I keep my jewelry.   OR   That is drawer which/that/Ø I keep my jewelry in.   OR   That is the drawer in which I keep my jewelry.

EXERCISE 15, p. 277. *Using* WHEN *in adjective clauses.*
Note: The adjective clauses are underlined.
1. Monday is the day when we will come.   OR   The day that/Ø we will come is Monday.   OR   The day on which we will come is Monday.   **2.** 7:05 is the time when my plane arrives.   OR   7:05 is the time that/Ø my plane arrives.   OR   7:05 is the time at which my plane arrives.   **3.** July is the month when the weather is usually the hottest.   OR   July is the month that/Ø the weather is usually the hottest.   OR   July is the month in which the weather is usually the hottest.   **4.** 1960 is the year when the revolution took place.   OR   1960 is the year that/Ø the revolution took place.   OR   1960 is the year in which the revolution took place.

EXERCISE 16, p. 278. *Using* WHERE *and* WHEN *in adjective clauses.*
Note: The adjective clauses are underlined.
3. A cafe is a small restaurant where people can get a light meal.   **4.** Every neighborhood in Brussels has small cafes where customers drink coffee and eat pastries.   **5.** There was a time when dinosaurs dominated the earth.   **6.** The house where I was born and grew up was destroyed in an earthquake ten years ago.
7. Summer is the time of year when the weather is the hottest.   **8.** The miser hid his money in a place where it was safe from robbers.   **9.** There came a time when the miser had to spend his money.   **10.** His new shirt didn't fit, so Dan took it back to the store where he'd bought it.

EXERCISE 19, p. 280. *Using adjective clauses to modify pronouns.*

Possible completions: **2.** that is troubling me. **3.** he can turn to.
4. I can do. **5.** who can help you. **6.** she meets. **7.** she said.
8. the lecturer says. **9.** he says is the result of years of experience.
10. who is standing. **11.** we took last week. **12.** I took my freshman year.
13. who came late **14.** who were in the first three rows . . . who were in the
back of the room . . .

EXERCISE 21, p. 282. *Punctuating adjective clauses.*

Note: The adjective clauses are underlined.

3. *No commas — "who" can be changed to "that."*

4. Matthew, <u>who speaks Russian</u>, applied for the job. — *"who" cannot be changed to
that."*

5. *No commas — "which" can be changed to "that."*

6. Rice, <u>which is grown in many countries</u>, is a staple food throughout much of the
world. — *"which" cannot be changed to "that."*

7. *No commas — "who" can be changed to "that."*

8. Paul O'Grady, <u>who died two years ago</u>, was a kind and loving man. — *"who"
cannot be changed to "that."*

9. I have fond memories of my hometown, <u>which is situated in a valley</u>. — *"which"
can be changed to "that."*

10. *No commas —"which" cannot be changed to "that."*

11. The Mississippi River, <u>which flows south from Minnesota to the Gulf
of Mexico</u>, is the major commercial river in the United States. — *"which" can
be changed to "that."*

12. No commas — *"which" can be changed to "that."*

13. Mr. Brown, <u>whose son won the spelling contest</u>, is very proud of his son's
achievement. — *"whose" cannot be changed to "that."* [*Second sentence = no
commas.*]

14. Goats, <u>which were first tamed more than 9,000 years ago in Asia</u>, have provided
people with milk, meat, and wool since prehistoric times. — *"which" cannot be
changed to "that."*

15. *No commas — "which" can be changed to "that."*

EXERCISE 22, p. 283. *Punctuating adjective clauses.*

3. a. **4.** b. **5.** a. **6.** b.

EXERCISE 23, p. 283. *Punctuating adjective clauses.*

1. *(no change)*   **2.** We enjoyed Mexico City, where we spent our vacation.
3. An elephant, which is the earth's largest land mammal, has few natural enemies other than human beings.   **4.** *(no change)*   **5.** At the botanical gardens, you can see a Venus's-flytrap, which is an insectivorous plant.   **6.** *(no change)*
7. One of the most useful materials in the world is glass, which is made chiefly from sand, soda, and lime.   **8.** Glaciers, which are masses of ice that flow slowly over land, form in the cold polar regions and in high mountains.   **9.** *(no change)*
10. Petroleum, which some people refer to as black gold, is one of the most valuable resources in the world today.   **11.** You don't have to take heavy clothes when you go to Bangkok, which has one of the highest average temperatures of any city in the world.   **12.** *(no change)*   **13.** Child labor was a social problem in late eighteenth-century England, where unemployment in factories became virtual slavery for children.   **14.** *(no change)*   **15.** *(no change)* — The man, who was wearing a plaid shirt and blue jeans, was caught shortly after he had left the bank.   **16.** *(no change)* — The research scientist, who was well protected before she stepped into the special chamber holding the bees, was not stung — *(no change)*

EXERCISE 24, p. 285. *Using expressions of quantity in adjective clauses.*

2. Last night the orchestra played three symphonies, <u>one of which was Beethoven's Seventh</u>.   **3.** I tried on six pairs of shoes, <u>none of which I liked</u>.   **4.** The village has around 200 people, <u>the majority of whom are farmers</u>.   **5.** That company currently has five employees, <u>all of whom are computer experts</u>.   **6.** After the riot, over one hundred people were taken to the hospital, <u>many of whom had been innocent bystanders</u>.

EXERCISE 25, p. 285. *Using expressions of quantity in adjective clauses.*

Possible completions: **2.** which is bright red.   **3.** whom are runners.
4. which is advanced physics.   **5.** whom speaks French.   **6.** which were very expensive.   **7.** whom I had already met.   **8.** which are unoccupied.

EXERCISE 26, p. 286. *Using noun + OF WHICH.*

2. They own an original Picasso painting, <u>the value of which is more than a million dollars</u>.   **3.** I bought a magazine, <u>the title of which is *Contemporary Architectural Styles*</u>.   **4.** My country is dependent upon its income from coffee, <u>the price of which varies according to fluctuations in the world market</u>.   **5.** The genetic engineers are engaged in significant experiments, <u>the results of which will be published in the *Journal of Science*</u>.   **6.** The professor has assigned the students a research paper, <u>the purpose of which is to acquaint them with methods of</u> <u>scholarly inquiry</u>.

EXERCISE 27, p. 286. *Using* WHICH *to modify a whole sentence.*
2. My roommate never picks up after herself, <u>which irritates me</u>. **3.** Mrs. Anderson responded to my letter right away, <u>which I appreciated very much</u>. **4.** There's been an accident on Highway 5, <u>which means I'll be late to work this</u> <u>morning</u>. **5.** I shut the door on my necktie, <u>which was really stupid of me</u>. **6.** Sally lost her job, <u>which wasn't surprising</u>. **7.** She usually came to work late, <u>which upset her boss</u>. **8.** So her boss fired her, <u>which made her angry</u>. **9.** She hadn't saved any money, <u>which was unfortunate</u>. **10.** So she had to borrow some money from me, <u>which I didn't like</u>. **11.** She has found a new job, <u>which is lucky</u>. **12.** So she has repaid the money she borrowed from me, <u>which I appreciate</u>. **13.** She has promised herself to be on time to work every day, <u>which is a good idea</u>.

EXERCISE 28, p. 287. *Using* WHICH *to modify a whole sentence.*
Sample sentences: **2.** I couldn't go to the movies last night, which disappointed me. **3.** The taxi driver was speeding, which made me nervous. **4.** Sandra lied to her surpervisor, which shocked all of us. **5.** David called from the police station, which means he's probably in trouble. **6.** My best friend took me to dinner for my birthday, which was a pleasant surprise. **7.** David didn't keep his date with Maria, which made her very unhappy. **8.** A friend visited my ailing mother in her nursing home, which I appreciated very much. **9.** The workmen outside my window were making a lot of noise, which made it difficult for me to concentrate. **10.** A news reporter said that a hurricane might hit our coast, which bothered me so much that I couldn't get to sleep.

EXERCISE 29, p. 288. *Special adjective clauses.*
Note: Words already provided in the text are in italics.
Sample completions: **1.** My best friend has four *brothers, all of whom* are older than she is. **2.** She mailed the package *early, which was fortunate* because she had written down the wrong due date. **3.** I carpool to school with four *students,* *three of whom* live in my apartment building. **4.** The art director asked his staff for *ideas, none of which* he liked. **5.** The women at the gala were wearing a lot of *jewelry, the value of which* was astronomical. **6.** This school has many fine *teachers, some of whom* have taught here for more than 20 years. **7.** I often wore clothes made by my *mother, which made me* proud of her. **8.** The teenager delivered newspapers to earn *a little money, all of which* he spent on a new bicycle.

9. The boy with the curly hair has three *sisters, each of whom* has straight hair.

10. We've just bought a *new car, the inside of which* smells like leather.

11. The college student came home with a bag of dirty *clothes, some of which* had to go to a dry cleaner.　　**12.** A tidal wave struck Papua New Guinea *two days ago, which surprised* the rest of the world.

EXERCISE 30, p. 288. *Adjective clauses.*

Note: The adjective clauses are underlined.

2. The blue whale, <u>which can grow to 100 feet and 150 tons,</u> is considered the largest animal that has ever lived.　　**3.** The plane was met by a crowd of three hundred people, <u>some of whom had been waiting for more than four hours.</u>

4. In this paper, I will describe the basic process <u>by which raw cotton becomes cotton thread.</u>　　**5.** The researchers are doing case studies of people <u>whose families have a history of high blood pressure and heart disease</u> to determine the importance of heredity in health and longevity.　　**6.** At the end of this month, scientists at the institute will conclude their AIDS research, <u>the results of which will be published within six months.</u>　　**7.** According to many education officials, "math phobia" (that is, fear of mathematics) is a widespread problem <u>to which a solution must and can be found.</u>　　**8.** The art museum hopes to hire a new administrator <u>under whose direction it will be able to purchase significant pieces of art.</u>　　**9.** The giant anteater, <u>whose tongue is longer than 30 centimeters (12 inches),</u> licks up ants for its dinner.　　**10.** The anteater's tongue, <u>which can go in and out of its mouth 160 times a minute,</u> is sticky.

EXERCISE 33, p. 291. *Adjective phrases.*

Note: The adjective clauses are underlined.

2. The people <u>waiting for the bus in the rain</u> are getting wet.　　**3.** I come from a city <u>located in the southern part of the country</u>.　　**4.** The children <u>attending that school</u> receive a good education.　　**5.** The scientists <u>researching the causes of cancer</u> are making progress.　　**6.** The fence <u>surrounding our house</u> is made of wood.

7. They live in a house <u>built in 1890</u>.　　**8.** We have an apartment <u>overlooking the park</u>.

EXERCISE 34, p. 291. *Adjective phrases.*

2. Be sure to follow the instructions ~~that are~~ given at the top of the page.　　**3.** The rules ~~that~~ <u>allowing</u> public access to wilderness areas need to be reconsidered.

4. The photographs ~~which were~~ published in the newspaper were extraordinary.

5. There is almost no end to the problems ~~that~~ <u>facing</u> a head of state.　　**6.** The psychologists ~~who~~ <u>studying</u> the nature of sleep have made important discoveries.

7. The experiment ~~which was~~ conducted at the University of Chicago was successful.

8. Kuala Lumpur, ~~which is~~ the capital city of Malaysia, is a major trade center in Southeast Asia. **9.** Antarctica is covered by a huge ice cap ~~that~~ <u>containing</u> 70 percent of the earth's fresh water. **10.** When I went to Alex's house to drop off some paperwork, I met Jerry, ~~who is~~ his longtime partner. **11.** Our solar system is in a galaxy ~~that is~~ called the Milky Way. **12.** Two out of three people ~~who are~~ struck by lightning survive. **13.** Simon Bolivar, ~~who was~~ a great South American general, led the fight for independence early in the 19th century. **14.** Many of the students ~~who~~ <u>hoping</u> to enter the university will be disappointed because only one-tenth of those ~~who~~ <u>applying</u> for admission will be accepted. **15.** There must exist in a modern community a sufficient number of persons ~~who~~ <u>possessing</u> the technical skill ~~that is~~ required to maintain the numerous devices upon which our physical comforts depend. **16.** Many famous people did not enjoy immediate success in their early lives. Abraham Lincoln, ~~who was~~ one of the truly great presidents of the United States, ran for public office 26 times and lost 23 of the elections. Walt Disney, ~~who was~~ the creator of Mickey Mouse and the founder of his own movie production company, once was fired by a newspaper editor because he had no good ideas. Thomas Edison, ~~who was~~ the inventor of the light bulb and the phonograph, was believed by his teachers to be too stupid to learn. Albert Einstein, ~~who was~~ one of the greatest scientists of all time, performed badly in almost all of his high school courses and failed his first college entrance exam.

EXERCISE 35, p. 292. *Adjective phrases.*

Note: The adjective clauses are underlined.

2. Corn was one of the agricultural products <u>which/that were introduced to the European settlers by the Indians</u>. Some of the other products <u>which/that were introduced by the Indians</u> were potatoes, peanuts, and tobacco. **3.** He read *The Old Man and the Sea,* <u>which is a novel</u> <u>which/that was written by Ernest Hemingway</u>. **4.** Mercury, <u>which is the nearest planet to the sun</u>, is also the smallest of the nine planets <u>which/that orbit the sun</u>. **5.** The pyramids, <u>which are the monumental tombs of ancient Egyptian pharaohs</u>, were constructed more than 4,000 years ago. **6.** The sloth, <u>which is a slow-moving animal</u> <u>which/that is found in the tropical forests of Central and South America</u>, feeds entirely on leaves and fruit. **7.** Two-thirds of those <u>who are arrested for car theft</u> are under twenty years of age. **8.** St. Louis, Missouri, <u>which is known as "The Gateway to the West,"</u> traces its history to 1763, when Pierre Laclede, <u>who was a French fur trader</u>, selected this site on the Mississippi River as a fur-trading post. **9.** Any student <u>who does not want to go on the trip</u> should inform the office. **10.** I just purchased a volume of poems <u>that/which were written by David Keller, who is a contemporary poet</u> <u>who is known for his sensitive interpretations of human relationships</u>.

EXERCISE 36, p. 292.   *Adjective phrases.*

2. Baghdad, the capital of Iraq.   **3.** seismographs, sensitive instruments that measure the shaking of the ground.   **4.** The Dead Sea, the lowest place on the earth's surface, ...   **5.** Buenos Aires, the capital of Argentina.   **6.** lasers, devices that produce a powerful beam of light.   **7.** Mexico, the northernmost country in Latin America, ...   **8.** Nigeria, the most populous country in Africa, ...   **9.** Both Mexico City, the largest city in the Western Hemisphere, and New York City, the largest city in the United States . . . .   **10.** The mole, a small animal that spends its entire life underground, . . . the aardvark, an African animal that eats ants and termites, ...

EXERCISE 37, p. 293.   *Review: adjective clauses and phrases.*

2. Disney World, an amusement park located in Orlando, Florida, covers a large area of land that includes lakes, golf courses, campsites, hotels, and a wildlife preserve.

3. Jamaica, the third largest island in the Caribbean Sea, is one of the world's leading producers of bauxite, an ore from which aluminum is made.

4. Oceanographer Robert Ballard made headlines in 1985 when he discovered the remains of the *Titanic,* the "unsinkable" passenger ship that has rested on the floor of the Atlantic Ocean since 1912, when it struck an iceberg.

5. William Shakespeare's father, John Shakespeare, was a glove maker and town official who owned a shop in Stratford-upon-Avon, a town about 75 miles (120 kilometers) northwest of London.

6. The Republic of Yemen, an ancient land located at the southwest tip of the Arabian Peninsula, has been host to many prosperous civilizations, including the Kingdom of Sheba and various Islamic empires.

EXERCISE 38, p. 294.   *Error analysis: adjective clauses and phrases.*

1. One of the people who(m) I admire most is my uncle.   **2.** Baseball is the only sport I am interested in it.   **3.** My favorite teacher, Mr. Chu, he was always willing to help me after class.   **4.** It is important to be polite to people who live in the same building.   **5.** She lives in a hotel which/that is restricted to senior citizens.   **6.** My sister has two children, whose their names are Ali and Talal.   **7.** He comes from Venezuela, which is a Spanish-speaking country.   **8.** There are some people in the government who are trying to improve the lives of poor people.   **9.** I have some good advice for anyone who he wants to learn a second language.   **10.** My classroom is located on the second floor of Carver Hall, which is a large brick building in the center of the campus.   **11.** A myth is a story which/that expresses traditional beliefs   OR   A myth is a story expressing traditional beliefs.   **12.** There is an old legend (which is) told among people in my country about a man living in the seventeenth century <u>who</u> saved a village from destruction.   **13.** An old man <s>was</s> fishing next to me on the pier was muttering to himself.   OR   An old man <u>who</u> was fishing next to me . . . .   **14.** When I was a child, I was always afraid of the beggars <u>who</u> <s>they</s> went from house to house in my neighborhood.   **15.** At the national park, there is a path <u>which/that</u> leads to a spectacular waterfall.   OR   At the national park there is a path <u>leading</u> to a spectacular waterfall.   **16.** The road that we took <s>it</s> through the forest <s>it</s> was narrow and steep.   **17.** There are ten universities in Thailand, seven of <s>them</s> <u>which are located</u> in Bangkok, (<u>which</u> is) the capital city.   **18.** I would like to write about several <u>problems</u> (which) I have faced <s>them</s> since I <u>came</u> to the United <u>States</u>.   **19.** There is a small wooden screen <u>which/that</u> separates the bed from the rest of the room.   OR   There is a small wooden screen <u>separating</u> the bed . . . .   **20.** At the airport, I was waiting for some relatives <u>who(m)/that/Ø</u> I had never met <s>them</s> before.   OR   At the airport, I was waiting for some relatives. <s>which</s> I had never met them before.   **21.** It is almost impossible to find two persons <u>whose</u> <s>their</s> opinions are the same.   **22.** On the wall, there is a colorful poster which <s>it</s> consists of a group of young people who <u>are</u> dancing.   OR   On the wall, there is a colorful poster <s>which it</s> <u>consisting</u> of a group of young people <s>who</s> dancing.   **23.** The sixth member of our household is Alex, <s>that</s> (<u>who</u> is) my sister's son.   OR   The sixth member of our household is Alex, <s>that is</s> my sister's son.   **24.** Before I came here, I didn't have the opportunity to speak with people <u>whose native tongue is English</u>.

~~~~~~~~~~~~~~~~~
~~~~~~~~~~~~~~~~~

Chapter Fourteen: GERUNDS AND INFINITIVES, PART 1

EXERCISE 1, p. 298. *Preview.*
2. about leaving   3. of doing   4. for being   5. to having   6. from completing   7. about/of having   8. of studying   9. for helping   10. on knowing   11. in being   12. of living   13. for not going   14. in searching   15. for making   16. for not wanting   17. for washing . . . drying   18. to going   19. from running   20. to going

21. of clarifying　　**22.** of stealing　　**23.** of taking . . . keeping
24. to wearing　　**25.** to eating . . . (to) sleeping

EXERCISE 2, p. 300. *Using gerunds as the objects of prepositions.*
Sample completions:　**2.** for lending me his fishing rod.　**3.** about going to the
opera tonight.　**4.** to living in an apartment.　**5.** about having a headache.
6. for not wanting to go to the dentist.　**7.** for being late to class.　**8.** about
missing the bus.　**9.** in finding out about the landscape of Mars.　**10.** about/of
going to Singapore next year.　**11.** for being late.　**12.** to driving on the left
side of the road.　**13.** from going to the hockey game!　**14.** for taking care of
ordering the paper for the copier?　**15.** to going to visit my grandparents.
16. of stealing the car.　**17.** to working in the school office, she has a job typing
manuscripts for one of the professors.　**18.** for not writing sooner.　**19.** of
telling a lie.　**20.** from traveling long distances.

EXERCISE 3, p. 300. *Using gerunds as the objects of prepositions.*
Note: The prepositions and their gerund objects are underlined.
Possible responses: **1.** Yes, I had a good excuse　OR　No, I didn't have a good excuse
<u>for being</u> late for class yesterday.　**2.** Yes, I am looking forward　OR　No, I'm not
looking forward <u>to going</u> to Boston to visit my friends this weekend.　**3.** Yes, I
thanked him/her　OR　No, I didn't thank him/her <u>for picking up</u> my pen.　**4.** Yes,
I'm accustomed　OR　No, I'm not accustomed <u>to living</u> in a cold/warm climate.
5. Yes, I'm excited　OR　No, I'm not excited <u>about going</u> to Italy for a vacation.
6. Yes, I aplogized　OR　No, I didn't apologize <u>for interrupting</u> Talal while he was
speaking.　　**7.** Yes, all of the students participated　OR　No, all of the students
didn't participate <u>in doing</u> pantomimes.　**8.** Yes, I know who is responsible　OR
No, I don't know who is responsible <u>for breaking</u> the window.　**9.** Yes, I'm used
to　OR　No, I'm not used <u>to having</u> my biggest meal in the evening.　**10.** The
hot weather prevents me <u>from running</u> every morning.　**11.** Yes, Peter
complains　OR　No, Peter doesn't complain <u>about/of having</u> a lot of homework to do.
12. Yes, I blame Susan　OR　No, I don't blame Susan <u>for staying</u> home in bed sick
last week.　**13.** S/he went to a baseball game <u>instead of studying</u> grammar last
night.　**14.** I read the newspaper <u>in addition to studying</u> last night.

EXERCISE 4, p. 301. *Using gerunds as the objects of prepositions.*
Possible completions: **4.** by eating.　**5.** by drinking.　**6.** by looking it up
in a dictionary.　**7.** by watching TV.　**8.** by waving to me.　**9.** by calling

an exterminator.   **10.** by wagging her tail.   **11.** by sticking a knife in the toaster.   **12.** by coming home late at night.

EXERCISE 5, p. 302. *Verbs followed by gerunds.*
Note: Words already provided in the text are in italics.
Sample responses: **1.** Sam *enjoyed watching TV* last night.   **2.** Would you *mind opening the window?*   **3.** James *quit eating desserts.*   **4.** James *gave up eating desserts* for six months.   **5.** Will *finished eating dinner* before he went out to play.   **6.** After Will *got through eating dinner,* he ran out to play.
7. When it *stops raining,* we can go to the beach.   **8.** Why did you *avoid answering my question?*   **9.** I cannot *postpone doing my work* any longer.
10. I have *put off doing my work* as long as I can.   **11.** We *delayed leaving* on vacation because of the hurricane.   **12.** I must *keep working* or I won't get home until late tonight.   **13.** Ted *kept on working* through his lunch hour.
14. My sister must *consider getting a job* if she wants to redecorate her kitchen this year.   **15.** She really doesn't want to *think about getting a job.*   **16.** Let's *discuss going to a movie* this weekend.   **17.** We'll *talk about going to a movie* when we meet for dinner this evening.   **18.** David *mentioned going to a concert* instead of a movie.   **19.** Rita *suggested going on a picnic* if the weather is nice.
20. I *enjoy listening to music* in the evening.

EXERCISE 6, p. 303. *Verbs followed by gerunds.*
Possible completions: **2.** closing/opening   **3.** raining   **4.** running
5. taking/going on   **6.** studying   **7.** giving/having   **8.** laughing
9. hitting   **10.** going   **11.** doing/starting   **12.** making   **13.** going
14. taking   **15.** being

EXERCISE 9, p. 305. *Special expressions followed by* -ING.
Possible completions: **2.** understanding   **3.** doing   **4.** waiting
5. taking   **6.** listening   **7.** going   **8.** getting   **9.** making
10. watching   **11.** eating   **12.** traveling [*BrE:* travelling]
13. doing . . . ordering meals in a restaurant   **14.** going to museums and Broadway shows   **15.** understanding the lecturers when they speak too fast
16. going to class and studying English

EXERCISE 10, p. 306. *Special expressions followed by* -ING.
Sample responses: **1.** I have trouble remembering phone numbers.   **2.** I have been standing at this counter for ten minutes waiting for a sales person.   **3.** Anton had a hard time learning how to spell "Antarctica."   **4.** I enjoy sitting in the park

and thinking about my plans for the weekend.   **5.** The children have a good time playing in the sandbox at the playground.   **6.** I was lying in the shade of a large tree dreaming about faraway places.   **7.** I have trouble pronouncing Mr. Krzyzewski's name correctly.   **8.** The teenagers had fun singing and dancing at the local club.   **9.** I found someone studying at my usual desk at the library.   **10.** Jack spent 30 minutes chatting with Ellen instead of studying for his chemistry test.   **11.** Don't waste money trying to win the lottery.   **12.** I caught my brother taking my car without my permission.

EXERCISE 11, p. 307.   *Verb + gerund or infinitive.*

Possible completions: **3.** to get / look for   **4.** to complete / do / finish   **5.** playing   **6.** to lend   **7.** to call / come   **8.** to finish / do   **9.** holding / opening   **10.** to be . . . whispering / talking   **11.** getting . . . to wait   **12.** to use   **13.** to write   **14.** not to touch   **15.** being   **16.** to be   **17.** to know   **18.** to write [*also possible:* writing]   **19.** to keep   **20.** to pass / take   **21.** to deliver / mail   **22.** to mail   **23.** to find   **24.** to find   **25.** finding   **26.** finding   **27.** to take   **28.** taking

EXERCISE 12, p. 309.   *Verbs followed by infinitives.*

Note: The verbs and the infinitives which follow them are underlined.

Expected sentences: **2.** The secretary <u>asked me to give</u> this note to Sue.   I <u>was asked to give</u> this note to Sue.   **3.** My advisor <u>advised me to take</u> Biology 109.   I <u>was advised to take</u> Biology 109.   **4.** When I went to traffic court, the judge <u>ordered me to pay</u> a fine.   I <u>was ordered to pay</u> a fine.   **5.** The teacher <u>warned Greg to keep</u> his eyes on his own paper during the test.   During the test, Greg <u>was warned to keep</u> his eyes on his own paper.   **6.** During the test, the teacher <u>warned Greg not to look</u> at his neighbor's paper.   Greg <u>was warned not to look</u> at his neighbor's paper during the test.   **7.** At the meeting, the head of the department <u>reminded the faculty not to forget</u> to turn in their grade reports by the 15th.   The faculty <u>was reminded not to forget</u> to turn in their grade reports by the 15th.   **8.** Mr. Lee <u>told the children to be</u> quiet.   The children <u>were told to be</u> quiet.   **9.** The hijacker <u>forced the pilot to land</u> the plane.   The pilot <u>was forced to land</u> the plane.   **10.** When I was growing up, my parents <u>allowed me to stay</u> up late on Saturday night.   When I was growing up, I <u>was allowed to stay</u> up late on Saturday night.   **11.** The teacher <u>encouraged the students to speak</u> slowly and clearly.   The students <u>were encouraged to speak</u> slowly and clearly.   **12.** The teacher <u>expects the students to come</u> to class on time. The students <u>are expected to come</u> to class on time.

62

EXERCISE 13, p. 310. *Using infinitives to report speech.*

Note: Verbs and infinitives are underlined.

Expected responses: **2.** The general <u>ordered</u> the soldiers <u>to surround</u> the enemy. **3.** Nancy <u>asked</u> me <u>to open</u> the window.   **4.** Bob <u>reminded</u> me <u>not to forget</u> to take my book back to the library.   **5.** Paul <u>encouraged</u> me <u>to take</u> singing lessons. **6.** Mrs. Anderson <u>warned</u> the children sternly <u>not to play</u> with matches.   **7.** The Dean of Admissions <u>permitted</u> me <u>to register</u> for school late.   **8.** Every driver <u>is required</u> by law <u>to have</u> a valid driver's license.   **9.** My friend <u>advised</u> me <u>to get</u> some automobile insurance.   **10.** The robber <u>forced</u> me <u>to give</u> him all my money. **11.** Before the examination began, the teacher <u>advised</u> the students <u>to work</u> quickly.   **12.** My boss <u>told</u> me <u>to come</u> to the meeting ten minutes early.

EXERCISE 14, p. 310. *Common verbs followed by infinitives.*

Note: Words already provided in the text are in italics.

Sample responses: **1.** Juan *reminded me to finish* washing the dishes before I left. I *was reminded to finish* washing the dishes before I left.   **2.** The teacher *asked me to go* to the front of the classroom. I *was asked to go* to the front of the classroom.   **3.** The ticket *permitted me to have* two free glasses of wine at the art show.   I *was permitted to have* two free glasses of wine at the art show.   **4.** My family *expected me to be* at the station when their train arrived. I *was expected to be* at the station when my family's train arrived.   **5.** The park ranger *warned me not to go* into the national forest alone. *I was warned not to go* into the national forest alone.   **6.** He also *advised me to take* a bottle of water and a compass. I *was* also *advised to take* a bottle of water and a compass.   **7.** My employer *told me to open* the mail by 11:00 every morning. I *was told to open* the mail by 11:00 every morning.   **8.** My doctor *encouraged me to visit* a warm, dry climate. I was *encouraged to visit* a warm, dry climate.   **9.** Our teacher *requires us to take* a test every week. We are required to *take* a test every week.

EXERCISE 15, p. 312. *Gerund vs. infinitive.*

2. to leave/leaving   **3.** to lecture/lecturing   **4.** to swim/swimming
5. to see/seeing   **6.** to move/moving . . . to race/racing . . . to move . . . to race
7. driving . . . taking   **8.** to drive . . . (to) take   **9.** to turn   **10.** being
11. to give   **12.** playing   **13.** doing   **14.** to do   **15.** to do
16. carrying   **17.** watching   **18.** to do   **19.** to inform   **20.** not
listening   **21.** to explain   **22.** holding . . . feeding . . . burping . . . changing

EXERCISE 16, p. 314. *Gerund vs. infinitive.*

2. cleaning   **3.** to take   **4.** to leave   **5.** talking/to talk   **6.** waiting . . . doing   **7.** to stay . . . (to) paint   **8.** quitting . . . opening   **9.** to take **10.** looking . . . to answer   **11.** postponing   **12.** watching . . . listening **13.** to read/reading   **14.** to go to camp / to go camping   **15.** singing **16.** to take . . . to pay   **17.** to stand   **18.** not to wait

EXERCISE 17, p. 315. *Gerund vs. infinitive.*

Note: Words already provided in the text are in italics.

Sample responses: **1.** (Ben) *reminded* me *to finish* polishing the car with a soft cloth.   **2.** *We* always *had fun swimming* at the lake every summer. **3.** *Students are required to have* two pencils for the exam.   **4.** *The counselor advised* Sharon *to take* an introductory math class.   **5.** *I am trying to learn* French.   **6.** (Our parents) *warned* us *not to open* the door to strangers. **7.** *I like to go camping* in the Rocky Mountains.   **8.** (Robert) *was invited to go* mountain climbing.   **9.** (He) *promised not to tell* Gloria's mother that Gloria had cut class.   **10.** *We aren't permitted to take* dogs into the student cafeteria. **11.** *My friend was asked to tell* our book club about the latest bestseller. **12.** *When the wind began to blow,* we flew our kite.   **13.** *I must remember to call* my Dad tonight.   **14.** (Mary) *told me not to worry about not being* dressed up for the dance.   **15.** (Frank) *was told to be* at the theater by 7:30 to get a good seat.   **16.** *I spent* five hours *writing* my last composition.

EXERCISE 19, p. 316. *Gerund vs. infinitive.*

1. talking   **2.** to play . . . not to make   **3.** to look after   **4.** paying **5.** to chase   **6.** going . . . to go   **7.** going skiing   **8.** not to smoke **9.** not to know/not knowing   **10.** whistling . . . to concentrate   **11.** doing **12.** to quit . . . (to) look for   **13.** to turn off   **14.** to renew **15.** not to wait   **16.** not to play   **17.** to call   **18.** convincing **19.** to throw away . . . (to) buy   **20.** dropping out of . . . hitchhiking . . . trying to find   **21.** to tell . . . to call . . . going swimming   **22.** to ask . . . to tell . . . to remember to bring

EXERCISE 20, p. 320. *Gerund vs. infinitive.*

1.	doing it.	**11.**	to do it.	**21.**	to do it?	**31.**	doing it.	**41.**	doing it.
2.	to do it.	**12.**	to do it.	**22.**	doing it?	**32.**	to do it.	**42.**	to do it.
3.	to do it.	**13.**	to do it.	**23.**	doing it?	**33.**	to do it.	**43.**	doing it.
4.	to do it.	**14.**	doing it.	**24.**	to do it.	**34.**	to do it.	**44.**	to do it.
5.	to do it.	**15.**	to do it.	**25.**	doing it.	**35.**	doing it.	**45.**	to do it.
6.	doing it.	**16.**	to do it.	**26.**	doing it.	**36.**	to do it.	**46.**	doing it?
7.	doing it.	**17.**	to do it.	**27.**	to do it.	**37.**	to do it.	**47.**	to do it.
8.	to do it.	**18.**	to do it.	**28.**	doing it.	**38.**	doing it.	**48.**	doing it?
9.	doing it.	**19.**	doing it.	**29.**	to do it.	**39.**	doing it?	**49.**	to do it?
10.	doing it.	**20.**	to do it.	**30.**	doing it?	**40.**	doing it.	**50.**	to do it.

EXERCISE 21, p. 321. *Gerund vs. infinitive.*

1. to bring   **2.** pronouncing   **3.** to eat   **4.** to hang up   **5.** to pull
6. to know   **7.** being   **8.** telling   **9.** to be   **10.** to do
11. to return . . . (to) finish   **12.** worrying   **13.** to play   **14.** telling
15. taking   **16.** to buy   **17.** to change   **18.** to have   **19.** being
20. hearing   **21.** promising to visit   **22.** to race   **23.** hoping . . .
praying   **24.** to persuade . . . to stay . . . (to) finish

EXERCISE 24, p. 323. IT + *infinitive.*

Note: The infinitives are underlined.

Sample sentences: **2.** It's important to look both ways before crossing a busy street.   **3.** It's not easy to learn a foreign language.   **4.** It's foolish to dive into water before checking its depth.   **5.** It must be interesting to be a foreign correspondent.   **6.** It's always a pleasure to see you.   **7.** It was clever of you to grasp the significance of the president's speech so quickly.   **8.** It doesn't cost much money to belong to a record club.   **9.** It's necessary to have a visa before you can travel to certain countries.   **10.** It takes time to learn how to play a musical instrument.

EXERCISE 25, p. 323. IT + *infinitive.*

Sample sentences: **2.** It's easy for Maria to speak Spanish because it's her native language.   OR   It's easy for someone to speak Spanish if s/he learns it as a child.   **3.** It's important for Toshi to learn English because he wants to attend an American university.   OR   It's important for someone to learn English if s/he plans to work at a foreign embassy.   **4.** It's essential for international students to get a visa if they plan to study here.   OR   It's essential for someone to get a visa if s/he wants to visit Russia.   **5.** It's important for engineering students to take advanced

math courses.   OR   It's important for someone studying engineering to take advanced math courses.   **6.** It's difficult for me to communicate with Mr. Wang.   OR   It's difficult for someone who does not know sign language to communicate with a deaf person.   **7.** It is impossible for Abdul to come to class because he is in the hospital.   OR   It is impossible for someone to come to class if s/he is out of town.
8. It's a good idea for us to study gerunds and infinitives because we get to practice ways of connecting ideas.   OR   It's a good idea for someone who wants to speak English fluently to study gerunds and infinitives.

EXERCISE 26, p. 324.   Gerunds as subjects.
Sample completions: **2.** Skiing down a steep mountain slope is hard.
3. Meeting new people can be interesting.   **4.** Visiting Prague was a good experience.   **5.** Does climbing a mountain with a pack on your back sound like fun to you?   **6.** Raising children demands patience and a sense of humor.
7. Rebuilding an engine is a complicated process.   **8.** Standing too close to a stranger is considered impolite in my country.

EXERCISE 27, p. 324.   IT + *infinitive; gerunds as subjects.*
Sample responses: **1.** It's dangerous to climb a mountain. Mountain climbing is dangerous.   **2.** It's easy to ride a bike. Riding a bike is easy.   **3.** It's impolite to interrupt someone.   Interrupting someone is impolite.   **4.** It is important to keep the peace. Keeping the peace is important.   **5.** It is wrong to drive through a stop sign. Driving through a stop sign is wrong.   **6.** It takes a lot of time to do a job well. Doing a job well takes a lot of time.   **7.** It's a good idea to park your car close to the curb. Parking your car close to the curb is a good idea.   **8.** Is it difficult to learn a foreign language? Is learning a foreign language difficult?

~~~~~~~~~~~~~~~~~
~~~~~~~~~~~~~~~~~

Chapter Fifteen: GERUNDS AND INFINITIVES, PART 2

EXERCISE 1, p. 326. *Error analysis:* IN ORDER TO.

2. Helen borrowed my dictionary ~~for~~ to look up the spelling of "occurred."

3. The teacher opened the window <u>to let</u> some fresh air in the room.   **4.** I came to this school <u>to</u> learn English.   **5.** I traveled to Osaka ~~for~~ to visit my sister.

EXERCISE 2, p. 327. IN ORDER TO *vs.* FOR.

Sample completions: **3.** bread and coffee.   **4.** buy some groceries.   **5.** have my annual checkup.   **6.** a smallpox inoculation.   **7.** stay in (good physical) shape.   **8.** exercise and recreation.   **9.** buy gas.   **10.** gas.

EXERCISE 3, p. 327. IN ORDER TO.

3. Ø   **4.** in order   **5.** in order   **6.** in order   **7.** Ø   **8.** in order
9. Ø   **10.** in order   **11.** in order   **12.** in order   **13.** Ø
14. in order   **15.** Ø

EXERCISE 4, p. 328. *Adjectives followed by infinitives.*

Possible completions: **2.** careful to lock my doors.   **3.** ready to go home.
4. eager to see my relatives again.   **5.** fortunate to have my family.   **6.** ashamed to ask anyone for a loan.   **7.** determined to succeed.   **8.** hesitant to accept it without the support of his wife and children.   **9.** delighted to accept the invitation.
10. shocked to learn that he had actually gotten a job!

EXERCISE 5, p. 329. *Adjectives followed by infinitives.*

1. Yes. (Maria) is fortunate to have a lot of good friends.   **2.** Yes. I'm eager to go on vacation.   **3.** Yes. I was delighted to meet Alice's husband.   **4.** Yes. I went to (Iceland) last summer. I was surprised to see Omar there too.   **5.** Yes. I am prepared to take the test tomorrow.   **6.** Yes. I am hesitant to ask (Yoko) a personal question.   **7.** Yes. I was relieved to find out that (Emily) was okay.
8. Yes. I was sorry to hear about (Jamal)'s accident.

EXERCISE 7, p. 330. *Using infinitives with* TOO *and* ENOUGH.

Possible completions: **3.** I don't want to watch a video. It's too late to start watching a video.   **4.** I don't want to take a walk. It's too cold to take a walk.
5. I don't understand nuclear physics. Nuclear physics is too difficult to understand.

6. I can't read Jenny a story. I'm too busy to read Jenny a story.   7. My son can't stay home alone. My son is too young to stay home alone.   8. I can't climb the mountain. The mountain cliff is too steep to climb.   10. I can walk the dogs. I'm very tired, but I'm not too tired to walk the dogs.   11. I can carry my suitcase. My suitcase is very heavy, but it's not too heavy for me to carry.   12. I can talk to you for a few minutes. I'm very busy, but I'm not too busy to talk to you for a few minutes.

EXERCISE 9, p. 332. *Passive and past forms of infinitives and gerunds.*
  4. to be invited   **5.** being understood   **6.** to be written   **7.** being hit
  8. to be called   **9.** being elected   **10.** to have lost   **11.** being told
  12. to be loved . . . needed   **13.** not having written / not writing
  14. having met / meeting   **15.** having been injured / being injured
  16. to have escaped   **17.** having gone / going   **18.** to have been invited

EXERCISE 10, p. 333. *Using gerunds or passive infinitives following* NEED.
  2. to be changed / changing   **3.** to be cleaned / cleaning . . . to clean   **4.** to be ironed / ironing   **5.** to be repaired / repairing   **6.** to take . . . to be straightened / straightening   **7.** to be picked / picking   **8.** to be washed / washing

EXERCISE 12, p. 334. *Using a passive to modify a gerund.*
  3. We greatly appreciate your (you) taking the time to help us.   **4.** The boy resented our (us) talking about him behind his back.   **5.** Their [*very informal:* Them] running away to get married shocked everyone.   **6.** I will no longer tolerate your (you) being late to work every morning.   **7.** Sally complained about Ann's (Ann) borrowing her clothes without asking her first.   **8.** We should take advantage of Helen's (Helen) being here to answer our questions about the company's new insurance plan.

EXERCISE 13, p. 335. *Review: verb forms.*
  1. to be asked   **2.** drinking   **3.** washing   **4.** to relax   **5.** to answer
  6. telling   **7.** beating   **8.** not being   **9.** to be awarded   **10.** to accept
  11. getting . . . (in order) to help   **12.** to travel . . . leave   **13.** Helping
  14. to be liked . . . trusted   **15.** wondering   **16.** to be chosen / to have been chosen   **17.** Living   **18.** doing . . . to interrupt   **19.** to take   **20.** to let
  21. to cooperate   **22.** hanging   **23.** to turn   **24.** hearing / having heard   **25.** leaving . . . going . . . (in order) to study   **26.** asking / having asked

27. driving . . . to drive   **28.** falling   **29.** (in order) to get   **30.** not being / not having been

EXERCISE 15, p. 337. *Using verbs of perception.*
PART I.   (*Possible completions.*)   **2.** sing/singing   **3.** walk/walking
4. shake/shaking   **5.** knock/knocking   **6.** take off/taking off . . . land/landing

PART II.   (*Expected completions.*)   **2.** slam   **3.** snoring   **4.** playing
5. call   **6.** walking   **7.** calling   **8.** play   **9.** singing . . . laughing
10. land   **11.** burning   **12.** touch

EXERCISE 17, p. 339. *Using the simple form after* LET *and* HELP.
Possible completions: **2.** correct our own quizzes.   **3.** borrow your
sweater?   **4.** tell you what to do.   **5.** (to) find his mother in the supermarket.
6. (to) locate the registrar's office. [*Note: omitting "to" is preferable stylistically.*
7. interrupt you.   **8.** (to) figure out how to operate this computer?

EXERCISE 18, p. 340. *Causative verbs.*
3. write   **4.** wash   **5.** to clean   **6.** cashed   **7.** to go   **8.** shortened
9. redo   **10.** filled   **11.** to lend   **12.** removed   **13.** cleaned
14. cry   **15.** to do   **16.** take

EXERCISE 19, p. 341. *Causative verbs.*
Possible completions: **2.** go to bed when they don't want to.   **3.** bring us a
wine list.   **4.** changed.   **5.** write on the chalkboard.   **6.** (to) move into a new
apartment.   **7.** print out two copies of my itinerary.   **8.** laugh.   **9.** go
downtown alone.   **10.** to replace our old refrigerator.

EXERCISE 21, p. 341. *Error analysis: gerunds, infinitives, causatives.*
1. Stop <u>telling</u> me what to do! Let me <s>to</s> make up my own mind.   **2.** My English is
pretty good, but sometimes I have trouble <s>to</s> <u>understanding</u> lectures at school.
3. When I entered the room, I found my wife <s>to</s> <u>crying</u> over the broken vase that had
belonged to her great-grandmother.   **4.** Sara is going to spend next year <s>for</s>
studying Chinese at a unversity in Taiwan.   **5.** I went to the pharmacy <u>to have</u> my
prescription <s>to be</s> filled.   **6.** You shouldn't let children <u>play</u> with matches.
7. When I got home, Irene was lying in bed <u>thinking</u> about what a wonderful time
she'd had.   **8.** When Shelley needed a passport photo, she had her picture <u>taken</u> by a
professional photographer.   **9.** I've finally assembled enough Information
<u>to begin</u> writing my thesis.   **10.** Omar is at the park right now. He is <u>sitting</u> on a

park bench <u>watching</u> the ducks <u>swimming</u> in the pond.   The sad expression on his face makes me ~~to~~ feel sorry for him.

EXERCISE 22, p. 342. *Review: verb forms.*
   2. trickling   **3.** to ignore   **4.** drink   **5.** move   **6.** play . . . joining
   7. being elected   **8.** to be told   **9.** have . . . join   **10.** drive
   11. sipping . . . eating   **12.** to let . . . run   **13.** make   **14.** talking
   15. being forced / to be forced to leave . . . to study . . . having   **16.** being
   17. to have . . . to know . . . to handle   **18.** Looking . . . realize . . . to be
   19. staying . . . getting   **20.** having . . . adjusting

EXERCISE 23, p. 343. *Review: verb forms.*
   1. being allowed   **2.** Observing . . . climbing/climb . . . realize (that)
   3. being surprised . . . planning   **4.** to have been performed   **5.** to be
   identified   **6.** to pick   **7.** having met/meeting . . . to be introduced   **8.** to have
   been considered/to be considered   **9.** to sleep . . . thinking   **10.** to force . . .
   to use . . . to feel . . . share   **11.** being accepted . . . concentrating   **12.** to
   persuade . . . to give . . . to cut . . . working . . . to retire . . . take . . . being dedicated
   13. to commute . . . moving . . . to give . . . to live . . . to be . . . doing . . . doing
   14. feel . . . to get . . . feeling . . . sneezing . . . coughing . . . to ask . . . to see . . . go
   15. chewing . . . grabbing . . . holding . . . tearing . . . swallow   **16.** to get . . .
   running . . . having . . . sprayed   **17.** being treated . . . threatening to stop
   working . . . to listen   **18.** being . . . being . . . to be understood . . . to bridge . . .
   teaching

EXERCISE 24, p. 345. *Error analysis: gerunds, infinitives, causatives.*
   1. My parents made me ~~to~~ promise to write them once a week.   **2.** I don't
   mind ~~to~~ <u>having</u> a roommate.   **3.** Most students want <u>to</u> return home as soon as
   possible.   **4.** When I went ~~to~~ shopping last Saturday, I saw a man ~~to~~ drive his car
   onto the sidewalk.   **5.** I asked my roommate to let me ~~to~~ use his shoe polish.
   6. ~~To~~ <u>Learning</u> about another country ~~it~~ is very interesting.   OR   It is very
   interesting to learn about another country.   **7.** I don't enjoy ~~to~~ <u>playing</u> card
   games.   **8.** I heard a car door ~~to~~ open and <u>close</u>. OR I heard a car door
   ~~to~~ <u>opening</u> and closing.   **9.** I had my friend ~~to~~ lend me his car.   **10.** I tried very
   hard <u>not to</u> make any mistakes.   OR   I tried very hard to ~~don't~~ make <u>no</u> mistakes.
   11. You should visit my country. It is <u>very</u> beautiful.   **12.** The music director
   tapped his baton <u>to begin</u> the rehearsal.   **13.** Some people prefer ~~to~~ <u>saving</u> their
   money to <u>spending</u> it. OR   Some people prefer to save their money <u>than</u> to spend it.
   14. The task of <u>finding</u> a person who could help us wasn't difficult.   **15.** All of us

needed to <u>go</u> to the cashier's window.   **16.** I am looking forward to <u>going</u> ~~to~~ <u>swimming</u> in the ocean.   **17.** When <u>you're</u> planting a garden, it's important to ~~be~~ <u>know</u> about soils.   **18.** My mother always <u>makes</u> me ~~to be~~ slow down if she <u>thinks</u> I am driving <u>too</u> fast.   **19.** One of our fights ended up with my/me having to <u>be</u> sent to the hospital <u>for/to get</u> stitches.   **20.** Please promise not <u>to tell</u> anybody my secret.   **21.** I would appreciate ~~having~~ <u>hearing</u> from you soon.   **22.** Maria has never complained about <u>having</u> a handicap.   **23.** Lillian deserves to be <u>told</u> the truth about what happened last night.   **24.** Barbara always makes me <u>laugh</u>. She has a great sense of humor.   **25.** Ali <u>doesn't</u> speak Spanish, and Juan <u>doesn't</u> know Arabic. But they communicate well by <u>speaking</u> Enlish when they <u>are</u> together. **26.** I enjoyed ~~to~~ <u>talking</u> to her on the phone. I look forward to <u>seeing</u> her next week. **27.** During a fire drill, everyone is required <u>to leave</u> the building.   **28.** <u>Skiing</u> in the Alps was a big thrill for me.   **29.** Don't keep ~~to be~~ <u>asking</u> me the same questions over and over.   **30.** When I entered the room, I found my young son <u>standing</u> on the kitchen table.

~~~~~~~~~~~~~~~~
~~~~~~~~~~~~~~~~

Chapter Sixteen: COORDINATING CONJUNCTIONS

EXERCISE 1, p. 348. *Parallel structure.*
   3. She spoke <u>angrily</u> and <u>bitterly</u> about the war. [adverb + adverb]
   4. I <u>looked</u> for my book but <u>couldn't find</u> it. [verb + verb]   **5.** I hope <u>to go</u> to that university and <u>study</u> under Dr. Liu. [infinitive + infinitive]   **6.** In my spare time, I enjoy <u>reading</u> novels or <u>watching</u> television. [gerund + gerund]   **7.** He <u>will leave</u> at eight and <u>arrive</u> at nine. [verb + verb]   **8.** He <u>should have broken</u> his engagement to Beth and <u>married</u> Sue instead. [verb + verb]

EXERCISE 2, p. 349. *Parallel structure.*
   2. Mary is opening the door and (is) greeting her guests.   **3.** Mary will open the door and (will) greet her guests.   **4.** Alice is kind, generous, and trustworthy.
   5. Please try to speak more loudly and clearly.   **6.** He gave her flowers on Sunday,

candy on Monday, and a ring on Tuesday.   7. While we were in New York, we attended an opera, ate at marvelous restaurants, and visited some old friends.   8. He decided to quit school, (to) go to California, and (to) find a job.   9. I am looking forward to going to Italy and eating wonderful pasta every day.   10. I should have finished my homework and (should have) cleaned up my room.   11. The boy was old enough to work and (to) earn some money.   12. He preferred to play baseball or (to) spend his time in the streets with other boys.   13. I like coffee but not tea. [*Note: Sometimes a comma precedes "but not": "I like coffee, but not tea."*]   14. I have met his mother (,) but not his father.   15. Jake would like to live in Puerto Rico (,) but not (in) Iceland.

EXERCISE 3, p. 350. *Parallel structure.*

Possible completions: 2. the food — I like to become acquainted with the people, (the) customs, and (the) food of other countries.   3. the noise — I dislike living in a city because of the air pollution, (the) crime, and (the) noise.
4. economic — We discussed some of the social, political, and economic problems of the United States.   5. a warm climate — Hawaii has a warm climate, many interesting tropical trees and flowers, and beautiful beaches.   6. is a good leader — Mary Hart would make a good president because she is a good leader, works effectively with others, and has a reputation for integrity and independent thinking.

EXERCISE 4, p. 351. *Parallel structure.*

Possible completions: 2. competent   3. said, "Good morning."   4. reading the newspaper   5. leave for work   6. Swimming at the lake   7. hiking on mountain trails   8. tolerant of those who are weak

EXERCISE 5, p. 351. *Error analysis: parallel structure.*

1. By obeying the speed limit, we can save energy, lives, and <u>money</u>.   2. My home offers me a feeling of security, <u>warmth</u>, and love.   3. The pioneers labored to clear away the forest and <u>plant</u> crops.   4. When I refused to help her, she became very angry and <u>shouted</u> at me.   5. In my spare time, I enjoy taking care of my aquarium and <u>working</u> on my stamp collection.   OR   In my spare time, I enjoy taking care of my aquarium and ~~to~~ <u>I</u> work on my stamp collection.   6. With their keen sight, fine hearing, and ~~they have a~~ refined sense of smell, wolves hunt elk, deer, moose, and caribou.   7. All plants need light, ~~to have~~ a suitable climate, and an ample supply of water and minerals from the soil.   8. Slowly and <u>cautiously</u>, the firefighter ascended the burned staircase.   9. The Indian cobra snake and the king cobra use poison from their fangs in two ways: by injecting it directly into their prey or ~~they~~ <u>(by) spitting</u> it into the eyes of the victim.   10. On my vacation, I lost a

suitcase, broke my glasses, and ╶┼╴ missed my flight home.   **11.** When Anna moved, she had to rent an apartment, make new friends, and ~~to~~ find a job.

EXERCISE 6, p. 352. *Error analysis: parallel structure.*

What do people in your country think of bats? Are they mean and scary creatures, or are they symbols of happiness and <u>luck</u>?

In Western countries, many people have an unreasoned fear of bats. According to scientist Dr. Sharon Horowitz, bats are <u>beneficial and harmless mammals</u>. "When I was a child, I believed that a bat would attack me and <u>tangle</u> itself in my hair. Now I know better," said Dr. Horowitz.

Contrary to popular Western myths, bats do not attack humans and <u>are</u> not blind. Although a few bats may be infected, they are not major carriers of rabies or ~~carry~~ other dread diseases. Bats help natural plant life by pollinating plants, spreading seeds, and ~~they~~ <u>eating</u> insects. If you get rid of bats that eat overripe fruit, then fruit flies can flourish and <u>destroy</u> the fruit industry.

According to Dr. Horowitz, bats make loving, ~~pets, and they are~~ trainable, and ~~are~~ gentle pets. Not many people, however, are known to have bats as pets, and bats themselves prefer to avoid people.

EXERCISE 7, p. 353. *Paired conjunctions.*

2. is   **3.** is   **4.** are   **5.** is   **6.** are   **7.** are   **8.** are

EXERCISE 8, p. 353. *Error analysis: paired conjunctions.*

Note: The paired conjunctions are underlined.

1. John will call <u>either Mary or Bob</u>. OR <u>Either John or Bob</u> will call Mary.
2. Sue saw <u>not only the mouse but also the cat</u>. OR Not only Sue <u>but (also) the cat</u> saw the mouse.   **3.** <u>Both my mother and (my) father</u> talked to the teacher. OR My mother talked to <u>both my teacher and my father</u>.   **4.** Either Mr. Anderson or Ms. Wiggins <u>is</u> going to teach our class today.   **5.** I enjoy reading <u>not only novels but also magazines</u>.   **6.** Oxygen is plentiful. Air contains <u>both oxygen and water</u>.

EXERCISE 9, p. 354. *Paired conjunctions.*

PART I.   **2.** Yes, <u>both the driver and the passenger</u> were injured in the accident.
3. Yes, <u>both wheat and corn</u> are grown in Kansas.   **4.** Yes, he <u>both buys and sells</u> used cars.   **5.** Yes, I had <u>both lunch and dinner</u> with my friends.   **6.** Yes, the city suffers from <u>both air (pollution) and water pollution</u>.

PART II.   **8.** Yes, <u>not only his cousin but also his mother-in-law</u> **is** living with him.   **9.** Yes, <u>not only my country but also the United States</u> **has** good universities.   **10.** Yes, I lost <u>not only my wallet but also my keys</u>.   **11.** Yes, she <u>not only goes</u> to school <u>but also has</u> a full-time job.   **12.** Yes, he bought <u>not only a coat but also a new pair of shoes</u>.

PART III.   **14.** Yes, I'm going to give my friend <u>either a book or a pen</u> for her birthday.   **15.** Yes, <u>either my sister or my brother</u> will meet me at the airport.   **16.** Yes, they can <u>either go swimming or play tennis</u>.   **17.** Yes, I'm going to vote for <u>either Mr. Smith or Mr. Jones</u>.   **18.** Yes, I'll go to <u>either New Orleans or Miami</u> for my vacation.

PART IV.   **20.** <u>Neither her husband nor her children</u> **speak** English.
21. <u>Neither the students nor the teacher</u> **is** wide awake today.   **22.** They have <u>neither a refrigerator nor a stove</u> for their new apartment.   **23.** She enjoys <u>neither hunting nor fishing</u>.   **24.** The result was <u>neither good nor bad</u>.

EXERCISE 10, p. 355. *Paired conjunctions.*
Note: The paired conjunctions are underlined.
2. <u>Both Ron and Bob</u> **enjoy** horseback riding.   OR   <u>Not only Ron but also Bob</u> **enjoys** horseback riding.   **3.** You can have <u>either tea or coffee</u>.   **4.** <u>Neither Arthur nor Ricardo</u> **is** in class today.   OR   <u>Not only Arthur but also Ricardo</u> **is** absent.
5. <u>Both Arthur and Ricardo</u> **are** absent.   **6.** We can <u>either fix</u> dinner for them here <u>or take</u> them to a restaurant.   **7.** She wants to buy <u>either a Chevrolet or a Toyota</u>.
8. <u>Both the leopard and the tiger</u> face extinction.   **9.** <u>Neither the library nor the bookstore</u> **has** the book I need.   **10.** We could <u>either fly or take</u> the train.
11. The president's assistant will <u>neither confirm nor deny</u> the story.   **12.** <u>Both coal and oil</u> **are** irreplaceable natural resources.   OR   <u>Not only coal but also oil</u> **is** an irreplaceable natural resource.   **13.** <u>Both smallpox and malaria</u> are dangerous diseases.   **14.** <u>Neither her roommates nor her brother</u> **knows** where she is.
15. According to the news report, it will <u>either snow or rain</u> tonight.

EXERCISE 11, p. 356. *Combining independent clauses with coordinating conjunctions.*
2. The teacher lectured**.** **T**he students took notes.   **3.** The teacher lectured**,** and the students took notes.   **4.** Elena came to the meeting**,** but Pedro stayed home.
5. Elena came to the meeting**.** **H**er brother stayed home.   **6.** Her academic record was outstanding**,** yet she was not accepted by the university.   **7.** I have not finished writing my term paper yet**.** **I** will not be finished until sometime next week.
8. *(no change)*   **9.** We had to go to the grocery store**,** for there was nothing in the house to fix for dinner.   **10.** Kostas didn't have enough money to buy an airplane ticket**,** so he couldn't fly home for the holiday.

74

EXERCISE 12, p. 356. *Combining independent clauses with coordinating conjunctions.*

1. A thermometer is used to measure temperature. **A** barometer measures air pressure.   **2.** Daniel made many promises, but he had no intention of keeping them.   **3.** I always enjoyed mathematics in high school, so I decided to major in it in college.   **4.** Anna is in serious legal trouble, for she had no car insurance at the time of the accident.   **5.** Last night Martha had to study for a test, so she went to the library.   **6.** The ancient Egyptians had good dentists. **Archaeologists** have found mummies that had gold fillings in their teeth.   **7.** Both John and I had many errands to do yesterday. John had to go to the post office and the bookstore. I had to go to the post office, the travel agency, and the bank.   **8.** I did not like the leading actor, yet the movie was quite good on the whole.   **9.** The team of researchers has not finished compiling the statistics yet. **Their** work will not be made public until later.   **10.** We have nothing to fear, for our country is strong and united.

11. He slapped his desk in disgust. **He** had failed another examination and had ruined his chances for a passing grade in the course.

12. I struggled to keep my head above water. I tried to yell for help, but **no sound** came from my mouth.

13. The earthquake was devastating. **Tall** buildings crumbled and fell to the earth.

14. It was a wonderful picnic. The children waded in the stream, collected rocks and insects, and flew kites. The teenagers played an enthusiastic game of **baseball.** The adults busied themselves preparing the food, supervising the children, and playing a game or two of volleyball.

15. Some people collect butterflies for a hobby. These collectors capture **them** with a net and put them in a jar that has poison in it. The dead butterflies are then mounted on a board.

16. Caterpillars eat plants and cause damage to some crops, but adult **butterflies feed** principally on nectar from flowers and do not cause any harm.

17. The butterfly is a marvel. It begins as an ugly caterpillar and turns into a work of art.

18. The sight of a butterfly floating from flower to flower on a warm sunny day brightens anyone's heart. **A** butterfly is a charming and gentle creature.

19. When cold weather comes, some butterflies travel great distances to reach tropical climates.

20. Butterflies are admired throughout the world because they are beautiful. **They** can be found on every continent except Antarctica.

~~~~~~~~~~~~~~~~~~

~~~~~~~~~~~~~~~~~~

Chapter Seventeen: ADVERB CLAUSES

EXERCISE 1, p. 360. *Adverb clauses.*

Note: The adverb clauses are underlined.

2. <u>When it began to rain</u>, he closed the windows.   **3.** He closed the windows <u>when it began to rain</u>.   **4.** <u>As soon as the rain began</u>, the children wanted to go outdoors. They love to play outside in the warm summer rain. I used to do the same thing <u>when I was a child</u>.   **5.** Jack got to the airport early. <u>After he checked in at the airline counter</u>, he went to the waiting area near his gate. He sat and read <u>until his flight was announced</u>.   **6.** Jack walked onto the plane, found his seat, and stowed his bag in an overhead compartment.   **7.** <u>Before the plane took off</u>, he fastened his seat belt and put his seat in an upright position.   **8.** Jack's wife doesn't like to fly <u>because she gets nervous on airplanes</u>.   **9.** <u>When Jack and his wife go on vacation</u>, they have to drive or take the train <u>because his wife is afraid of flying</u>.   **10.** I had a cup of tea <u>before I left for work this morning</u>, but I didn't have anything to eat. I rarely eat breakfast.   **11.** <u>After Ellen gets home from work</u>, she likes to read the newspaper. She follows the same routine every day after work. <u>As soon as she gets home</u>, she changes her clothes, gets a snack and a drink, and sits down in her favorite chair to read the newspaper in peace and quiet. She usually has about half an hour to read the paper <u>before her husband arrives home from his job</u>.

12. <u>When you speak to someone</u> [who is hard of hearing = *adjective clause*], you do not have to shout. It is important to face the person directly and speak clearly. My elderly father is hard of hearing, but he can understand me <u>if I face him, speak slowly, and say each word clearly</u>.

13. Greg Adams has been blind <u>since he was two years old</u>. Today he is a key scientist in a computer company. He is able to design complex electronic equipment <u>because he has a special computer</u> [that reads, writes, and speaks out loud = *adjective clause*]. His blindness neither helps nor hinders him. It is irrelevant to [how well he does his job = *noun clause*].

EXERCISE 2, p. 361. *Review of adverb clauses of time.*

Sample completions: **1.** Since I came to this city, I've met a lot of nice people.
2. Just as I was falling asleep last night, a mosquito buzzed in my ear and woke me up.   **3.** I'll help you with your homework as soon as I finish washing the dishes.
4. I was late. By the time I got to the airport, my plane had already taken off.
5. One of my friends gets nervous every time she has to perform in public.
6. I will be here until I have completed my education.   **7.** I will remember my

wedding day as long as I live. **8.** I heard the phone ring while I was in the shower.
9. Once summer comes, the traffic on the highway becomes heavier. **10.** Shortly
before I put supper on the table, the cat demanded to be fed. **11.** I have been in
this country for three years. By the time I leave, I will be able to speak English
fluently. **12.** The last time I was with my family, I was 24 years old.
13. The next time I see them, I'll be 28. **14.** I will be with you just as soon as
I finish checking this inventory. **15.** Not long after I bought the car, I ran
over a nail and got a flat tire. **16.** I had already finished supper when
you telephoned. **17.** Whenever I'm late for an important meeting, I get
nervous. **18.** Ever since I was a child, I've been afraid of snakes.

EXERCISE 3, p. 362. *Using adverb clauses to show cause and effect.*
Note: The adverb clauses are underlined.
3. Cold air hovers near the earth <u>because it is heavier than hot air</u>. **4.** <u>Since you
paid for the theater tickets,</u> please let me pay for our dinner. **5.** <u>Now that Larry is
finally caught up on his work,</u> he can start his vacation tomorrow. **6.** <u>Because
our TV set was broken,</u> we listened to the news on the radio. **7.** My brother got
married last month. <u>Now that he's a married man,</u> he has more responsibilities.
8. <u>Since oil is an irreplaceable natural resource,</u> we must do whatever we can in
order to conserve it. **9.** Do you want to go for a walk <u>now that the rain has
stopped</u>? **10.** Many young people move to the cities in search of employment <u>since
there are few jobs available in the rural areas</u>. **11.** <u>Now that the civil war has
ended,</u> a new government is being formed. **12.** <u>Since ninety-two thousand people
already have reservations with an airline company for a trip to the moon,</u> I doubt that
I'll get the chance to go on one of the first tourist flights.

EXERCISE 4, p. 363. *Using adverb clauses to show cause and effect.*
Note: The adverb clauses are underlined.
Sample completions: **1.** <u>Now that I've finally finished cleaning my room,</u> I can
watch TV. **2.** The teacher didn't collect the papers <u>because the exercise is not
going to be graded</u>. **3.** <u>Since it's too expensive to fly across the country,</u> we are
going by bus. **4.** Jack can't stay out all night with his friends <u>now that he is
married</u>. **5.** <u>Since we don't have class tomorrow,</u> we can stay up later tonight.

EXERCISE 5, p. 364. *Using* EVEN THOUGH.
3. even though **4.** because **5.** Even though **6.** Because **7.** even
though **8.** because **9.** even though **10.** even though
11. because **12.** Even though . . . because

EXERCISE 7, p. 365. *Using* EVEN THOUGH *and* BECAUSE.

Sample completions: **3.** Because it was a beautiful day, I went fishing.
4. Even though it was a work day, I went fishing.   **5.** Even though there were very few customers in the store, we decided to stay open until 9:00 P.M.   **6.** Because there were very few customers in the store, we closed early.   **7.** I wore heavy gloves because the temperature was below freezing.   **8.** Even though my feet were killing me and my head was pounding, I finished running the marathon.   **9.** Even though I was speeding, I didn't get a traffic ticket.   **10.** Even though I was tired, I finished my homework because my essay was due the next day.   **11.** Even though I didn't like baked beans when I was small, I always finished them because I wanted dessert.   **12.** Because we didn't have a television set while I was growing up, I watched TV at my neighbor's house even though my parents didn't approve.

EXERCISE 8, p. 366. *Using* WHILE *and* WHEREAS.
2. D.   **3.** C.   **4.** C.   **5.** B.   **6.** B.

EXERCISE 11, p. 368. *Using* WHETHER OR NOT *and* EVEN IF.
2. Sam laughs at the jokes:
    a. whether they're funny or not.   b. even if they're not funny.
3. You have to hand in your examination paper:
    a. whether you're finished or not.   b. even if you're not finished.
4. We're going to go camping in the mountains:
    a. whether it snows or not.   b. even if it snows.
5. Max can go to school:
    a. whether or not he gets a scholarship.   b. even if he doesn't get a scholarship.
6. My grandfather wears his gray sweater:
    a. whether or not the weather is cold.   b. even if the weather is hot.
7. I'm going to marry Harry:
    a. whether you approve or not.   b. even if you don't approve.

EXERCISE 12, p. 369. *Using* WHETHER OR NOT *and* EVEN IF.
Sample completions: **1.** We're not going to the park today even if the weather improves.   **2.** Even if she apologizes to her supervisor, Maria may lose her job.
3. Getting that job depends on whether or not you can speak English.   **4.** I'm going to help you whether you want me to or not.   **5.** I won't tell you even if you beg me.
6. I'm really angry! Maybe he'll apologize, and maybe he won't. It doesn't matter. Even if he tells me he's really sorry, I won't forgive him!   **7.** I'm exhausted. Please don't wake me up even if the house catches on fire.   **8.** I'm not going to buy

that sweater even if it is my favorite color.   9.   Even if it rains, I'm going to take my morning walk.   10.   I'm going to quit school whether my parents like it or not.

EXERCISE 13, p. 369. *Using* IN CASE *and* IN THE EVENT THAT.

2. In case / In the event that you need to see me, I'll be in my office tomorrow morning around ten.   3.   In case / In the event that you need more information, you can call me.   4.   In case / In the event that you have any more questions, ask Dr. Smith.   5.   In case / In the event that Jack calls, please tell him that I'm at the library.   6.   In case / In the event that you're not satisfied with your purchase, you can return it to the store.

Sample completions: 7.   . . . you'll have to go to the library.   8.   . . . you lose your credit cards.   9.   . . . my parents decide to come for a visit after all.
10.   . . . it rains.   11.   . . . the refugees can at last return to their homes.
12.   . . . please start without me.   13.   . . . it malfunctions.

EXERCISE 14, p. 370. *Using* UNLESS.

2. You can't travel abroad unless you have a passport.   3.   You can't get a driver's license unless you're at least sixteen years old.   4.   Unless I get some film, I won't be able to take pictures when Ann and Rob get here.   5.   You'll get hungry during class unless you eat breakfast.

EXERCISE 15, p. 371. *Using* UNLESS.

Sample completions: 2.   I'm sorry, but you can't see the doctor unless you have an appointment.   3.   I can't graduate from school unless I pass all my courses.
4. That food will spoil unless you put it in the refrigerator.   5.   Unless it rains, we plan to have the birthday party in the backyard.   6.   Certain species of animals will soon become extinct unless we stop destroying their habitats.   7.   I will have to look for another job unless I get a raise in salary.   8.   Tomorrow I'm going to call my sister unless I hear from her in today's mail.   9.   The political situation in (. . .) will continue to deteriorate unless the opposing sides commit to ending the hostilities and creating a lasting peace.   10.   He doesn't say anything unless the teacher calls on him.   11.   Unless you start doing your share of the housework, you'll have to look for another roommate.

EXERCISE 16, p. 371. *Using* ONLY IF.

2. You can go to the party only if you have an invitation.   3.   You can attend this school only if you have a student visa.   4.   Jimmy chews gum only if he's sure his mother won't find out.   5.   We will go to the movie only if you want to.   6.   Water will freeze only if the temperature reaches 32°F / 0°C.   7.   Only if you study hard

will you pass the exam.   **8.** Only if you have a ticket can you get into the soccer stadium.   **9.** Only if Jake's homework is finished can he watch TV in the evening.
10. Only if I get a job will I have enough money to go to school.
11. - 13. *(open completion)*

EXERCISE 17, p. 372. *Using* UNLESS *and* ONLY IF.
2. I can't pay my bills unless I get a job. I can pay my bills only if I get a job.
3. Your clothes will get clean only if you use soap. Your clothes won't get clean unless you use soap.   **4.** I can't take any pictures unless I buy some film. I can take pictures only if I buy some film.   **5.** I don't wake up unless the alarm clock rings. I wake up only if the alarm clock rings.   **6.** Eggs won't hatch unless they're kept at the proper temperature. Eggs will hatch only if they're kept at the proper temperature.   **7.** Don't borrow money from friends unless you absolutely have to. Borrow money from friends only if you absolutely have to.   **8.** Anna doesn't talk in class unless the teacher asks her specific questions. Anna talks in class only if the teacher asks her specific questions.

~~~~~~~~~~~~~~~~~
~~~~~~~~~~~~~~~~~

Chapter Eighteen: REDUCTION OF ADVERB CLAUSES TO MODIFYING ADVERBIAL PHRASES

EXERCISE 1, p. 375. *Changing time clauses to modifying adverbial phrases.*
3. Before _I_ came to class, _I_ had a cup of coffee. *Before coming to class,* I had a cup of coffee.   **4.** Before the student came to class, the teacher had already given a quiz. *(no change)*   **5.** Since _I_ came here, _I_ have learned a lot of English. *Since coming here,* I have learned a lot of English.   **6.** Since Bob opened his new business, he has been working 16 hours a day. *Since opening his new business,* Bob has been working 16 hours a day.   **7.** After Omar (had) finished breakfast, he left the house and went to his office. *After finishing / having finished breakfast,* Omar left the house and went to his office.   **8.** Alex hurt his back while he was chopping wood. Alex hurt his back *while chopping wood.*   **9.** You should always read a

contract before you sign your name. You should always read a contract *before signing your name.*   **10.** Before the waiter came to the table, I had already made up my mind to order shrimp. *(no change)*   **11.** Before you ask the librarian for help, you should make every effort to find the materials yourself. *Before asking the librarian for help,* you should make every effort to find the materials yourself.
12.   While Jack was trying to sleep last night, a mosquito kept buzzing in his ear. *(no change)*   **13.** While Susan was climbing the mountain, she lost her footing and fell onto a ledge several feet below. *While climbing the mountain,* Susan lost her footing and fell onto a ledge several feet below.   **14.** The Wilsons have experienced many changes in their lifestyle since they adopted twins. The Wilsons have experienced many changes in their lifestyle *since adopting twins.*
15. After I heard Mary describe how cold it gets in Minnesota in the winter, I decided not to go there for my vacation in January. *After hearing Mary describe how cold it gets in Minnesota in the winter,* I decided not to go there for my vacation in January.

EXERCISE 3, p. 377. *Modifying adverbial phrases.*
2. *Believing that no one loved him,* the little boy ran away from home.
3. *Not paying attention to where she was going,* Rosa stepped into a hole and sprained her ankle.   **4.** *Having forgotten to bring a pencil to the examination,* I had to borrow one.   **5.** *Being a vegetarian,* Chelsea does not eat meat.   **6.** *Having already flunked out of school once,* Mike is determined to succeed this time.

EXERCISE 4, p. 377. *Modifying adverbial phrases.*
1. *Before talking to you,* I had never understood that formula.   **2.** *Not wanting to spend any more money this month,* Larry decided against going to a restaurant for dinner.   **3.** *After reading the chapter four times,* I finally understood the author's theory.   **4.** *Remembering that everyone makes mistakes,* I softened my view of his seemingly inexcusable error.   **5.** *Since completing his Bachelor's degree,* he has had three jobs, each one better than the last.   **6.** *While traveling across the United States,* I could not help being impressed by the great differences in terrain.   **7.** *Before gaining national fame,* the union leader had been an electrician in a small town.   **8.** *Enjoying the cool evening breeze and listening to the sounds of nature,* we lost track of time.   **9.** *Having never flown in an airplane before,* the little girl was surprised and a little frightened when her ears popped.   **10.** *Before becoming vice-president of marketing and sales,* Peter McKay worked as a sales representative.

EXERCISE 5, p. 378. *Modifying adverbial phrases.*

2. *Hearing that Nadia was in the hospital,* I called her family to find out what was wrong. **3.** *(no change)* **4.** *Living a long distance from my work,* I have to commute daily by train. **5.** *Living a long distance from her work,* Heidi has to commute daily by train. **6.** *(no change)* **7.** *Not wanting to inconvenience my friend by asking her to drive me to the airport,* I decided to take a taxi. **8.** *Sitting on a large rock at the edge of a mountain stream,* I felt at peace with the world. **9.** *Being a married man,* I have many responsibilities. **10.** *Trying his best not to cry,* the little boy swallowed hard and began to speak. **11.** *Keeping one hand on the steering wheel,* Anna opened a can of soda pop with her free hand. **12.** *(no change)* **13.** *Recognizing his face but having forgotten his name,* I just smiled and said, "Hi." **14.** *(no change)* **15.** *(Being) Convinced that she could never learn to play the piano,* Anna stopped taking lessons.

EXERCISE 6, p. 378. *Modifying adverbial phrases.*

1. Having sticky pads on their feet, flies can easily walk on the ceiling. **2.** Having worked with computers for many years, Ed has an excellent understanding of their limitations as well as their potential. **3.** Having been born two months prematurely, Mary needed special care for the first few days of her life. **4.** Having done everything he could for the patient, the doctor left to attend other people. **5.** Having never eaten Thai food before, Sally didn't know what to expect when she went to the Thai restaurant for dinner. **6.** Having no one to turn to for help, Sam was forced to work out the problem by himself. **7.** Being an endangered species, rhinos are protected by law from poachers who kill them solely for their horns. **8.** Being able to crawl into very small spaces, mice can hide in almost any part of a house. **9.** Having done very well in her studies, Nancy expects to be hired by a top company after graduation. **10.** Being extremely hard and nearly indestructible, diamonds are used extensively in industry to cut other hard minerals.

EXERCISE 7, p. 379. *Modifying adverbial phrases.*

3. *(no change)* **4.** *Because I was too young to understand death,* my mother gave me a simple explanation of where my grandfather had gone. **5.** *(no change)* **6.** *While I was working in my office late last night,* someone suddenly knocked loudly at my door and nearly scared me to death! **7.** *After we (had) hurried to get everything ready for the picnic,* it began to rain just as we were leaving. **8.** *While I was walking across the street at a busy intersection,* a truck nearly ran over my foot.

82

EXERCISE 8, p. 380. *Using* UPON + -ING.

2. *Upon crossing* the marathon finish line, Tina fell in exhaustion. **3.** *Upon looking in my wallet,* I discovered I didn't have enough money to pay my restaurant bill. **4.** I bowed my head *upon meeting* the king. **5.** *Upon rereading* the figures, Sam found that he had made a mistake. **6.** . . . *Upon discovering* it was hot, the small child jerked his hand back, ... **7.** Mrs. Alexander nearly fainted *upon learning* that she had won the lottery. **8.** *Upon finishing* the examination, bring your paper to the front of the room. **9.** . . . *Upon hearing my name,* I raised my hand to identify myself. **10.** . . . *Upon hearing* this, Cook grabbed his telescope and searched the horizon.

EXERCISE 9, p. 381. *Review: modifying adverbial phrases.*

5. *Before leaving* on my trip, I checked to see what shots I would need.
6. *(no change)* **7.** *Not having understood* the directions, I got lost.
8. My father reluctantly agreed to let me attend the game *after having talked / talking* it over with my mother. **9.** *Upon discovering / Discovering* I had lost my key to the apartment, I called the building superintendent. **10.** *(no change)*
11. Garcia Lopez de Cardenas accidentally discovered the Grand Canyon *while looking* for the legendary Lost City of Gold. **12.** *(no change)* **13.** *After having to wait* for more than half an hour, we were finally seated at the restaurant.
14. *Before getting accepted* on her country's Olympic running team, Maria had spent most of the two previous years in training. **15.** *Not paying* attention to his driving, George didn't see the large truck until it was almost too late.

EXERCISE 10, p. 382. *Review: modifying adverbial phrases.*

1. . . . When Watson heard words coming from the machine, he immediately realized that their experiments had at last been successful.

    [Hearing words coming from the machine, = *adverb phrase*]

. . . After Bell had successfully tested the new apparatus again and again, he confidently announced his invention to the world.

    [After having / Having successfully tested the new apparatus again and again, = *adverb phrase*]

. . . Because they believed the telephone was a toy with little practical application, most people paid little attention to Bell's announcement.

    [Believing the telephone was a toy with little practical application, = *adverb phrase*]

2. . . . <u>Because many people believe that wolves eagerly kill human beings</u>, they fear them.

[Believing that wolves eagerly kill human beings, = *adverb phrase*]

. . . <u>Because they are strictly carniverous</u>, wolves hunt large animals . . . .

[Being strictly carniverous = *adverb phrase*]

. . . <u>Because it was relentlessly poisoned, trapped, and shot by ranchers and hunters</u>, the timber wolf, ...

[Having been / Being relentlessly poisoned, trapped, and shot by ranchers and hunters, = *adverb phrase*]

. . . In the 1970s, <u>after they realized a mistake had been made</u>, U. S. lawmakers passed laws to protect wolves.

[In the 1970s, after realizing / after having realized / having realized that a mistake had been made, = *adverb phrase*]

. . . Today, <u>after they have been unremittingly destroyed for centuries</u>, they are found in few places, ...

[Today, after having been / after being / having been unremittingly destroyed for centuries, = *adverb phrase*]

EXERCISE 11, p. 383. *Review: modifying adverbial phrases.*

Possible completions: **1.** After having finished my weeding, I decided to take a break before I mowed the lawn. **2.** Before going to Canada, I had never seen snow. **3.** Since coming to this school, I have learned a great deal about the English language. **4.** Sitting in the park the other day, Sharon saw a squirrel with a red tail. **5.** Having heard a strange noise in the other room, the babysitter decided to call a neighbor to help her investigate. **6.** Being new on the job, the sales clerk didn't know when to take his afternoon break. **7.** Being the largest city in the United States, New York has a considerable problem with homeless people. **8.** Upon reaching our destination, we leapt out of the car and ran toward the lake. **9.** Receiving no answer when he knocked on the door, the mailman took the registered package back to the post office. **10.** Exhausted by the long hours of work, the medical student was too tired to eat his dinner.

EXERCISE 12, p. 384. *Error analysis: general review.*

2. Because our leader could not attend the meeting, ~~so~~ it was canceled. OR ~~Because~~ Our leader could not attend the meeting, so it was canceled. **3.** <u>My wife and I like</u> to travel. **4.** I always fasten my seat belt before ~~to~~ starting the engine. OR I always fasten my seat belt before ~~to~~ <u>I</u> start the engine. **5.** I don't like our classroom **because** it is hot and crowded. I hope we can change to a different room. **6.** <u>Since / Because</u> the day was very warm and humid, ~~for that~~ I turned on the air conditioner.   7. Upon + <u>learning</u> that my car couldn't be repaired for three days, I <u>was</u> very distressed.   8. <u>Because</u> I missed the final examination <s>because</s>, the teacher gave me a failing grade.   9. Both my sister and (my) brother <u>are</u> going to be at the family reunion.   10. I hope my son will remain in school until he <u>finishes</u> his degree.   11. My brother has succeeded in business because <s>of</s> he works hard.   12. Luis stood up, turned toward me, and <u>spoke</u> so softly that I couldn't hear what he said.   13. I was lost. I could not find my parents <u>or</u> my brother.   OR I could <s>not</s> find <u>neither</u> my parents <u>nor</u> my brother.   14. <u>Since</u> she <u>had</u> studied Greek for several years, Sarah's pronunciation was easy to understand.

~~~~~~~~~~~~~~~~~
~~~~~~~~~~~~~~~~~

Chapter Nineteen: CONNECTIVES THAT EXPRESS CAUSE AND EFFECT, CONTRAST, AND CONDITION

EXERCISE 1, p. 385. *Preview.*
1. Because <s>of</s> Rosa's computer skills were poor, she was not considered for the job.
2. Rosa's computer skills were poor. Therefore, she was not considered for the job.   3. Because Rosa's computer skills were poor, <s>therefore</s> she was not considered for the job.   OR <s>Because</s> Rosa's computer skills were poor. Therefore, she was not considered for the job.   4. Because Rosa's computer skills were poor, <s>so</s> she was not considered for the job.   OR <s>Because</s> Rosa's computer skills were poor, so she was not considered for the job.   5. Due to her poor computer skills, Rosa was not considered for the job <s>therefore</s>.   6. <s>Consequently</s> Rosa's computer skills were poor. <u>Consequently,</u> she was not considered for the job.   OR <u>Because</u> Rosa's computer skills were poor, she was not considered for the job.

EXERCISE 2, p. 386. *Using* BECAUSE *and* BECAUSE OF.
3. because   4. because of   5. Because of   6. Because   7. because of
8. because of

EXERCISE 3, p. 386. *Using* BECAUSE OF *and* DUE TO.

2. the heavy traffic   **3.** his wife's illness   **4.** Dr. Robinson's excellent research on wolves   **5.** the noise in the next apartment   **6.** circumstances beyond my control

EXERCISE 4, p. 387. *Using* THEREFORE *and* CONSEQUENTLY.

1. A storm was approaching. Therefore, the children stayed home.

A storm was approaching. The children, therefore, stayed home.

A storm was approaching. The children stayed home, therefore.

2. I didn't have my umbrella. Consequently, I got wet.

I didn't have my umbrella. I, consequently, got wet.

I didn't have my umbrella. I got wet, consequently.

EXERCISE 5, p. 388. *Showing cause and effect.*

1. Because it was cold, she wore a coat.   **2.** *(no change)*   **3.** Because of the cold weather, she wore a coat.   **4.** *(no change)*   **5.** The weather was cold. Therefore, she wore a coat.   **6.** The weather was cold. She, therefore, wore a coat. **7.** The weather was cold. She wore a coat, therefore.   **8.** The weather was cold, so she wore a coat.

EXERCISE 6, p. 388. *Showing cause and effect.*

1. Pat always enjoyed studying sciences in high school. **Therefore,** she decided to major in biology in college.   **2.** Due to recent improvements in the economy, fewer people are unemployed.   **3.** Last night's storm damaged the power lines. **Consequently,** the town was without electicity for several hours.   **4.** Because of the snowstorm, only five students came to class. **The teacher, therefore,** canceled the class.   **5.** *(no change)*

EXERCISE 7, p. 389. *Showing cause and effect.*

PART I.   **2.** The weather was bad. <u>Therefore,</u> we postponed our trip.   OR   We, <u>therefore,</u> postponed our trip.   OR   We postponed our trip, <u>therefore</u>.   **3.** <u>Since</u> the weather was bad, we postponed our trip.   OR   We postponed our trip <u>since</u> the weather was bad.   **4.** The weather was bad, <u>so</u> we postponed our trip. **5.** <u>Because of</u> the bad weather, we postponed our trip.   OR   We postponed our trip <u>because of</u> the bad weather.   **6.** The weather was bad. <u>Consequently,</u> we postponed our trip.   OR   We, <u>consequently,</u> postponed our trip.   OR   We postponed our trip, <u>consequently</u>.   **7.** <u>Due to the fact that</u> the weather was bad, we postponed our trip. OR   We postponed our trip <u>due to the fact that</u> the weather was bad.

PART II.   **1.** <u>Because of</u> her illness, she missed class.   OR   She missed class <u>because of</u> her illness.   **2.** <u>Because</u> she was ill, she missed class.   OR   She missed class <u>because</u> she was ill.   **3.** She was ill. <u>Consequently,</u> she missed class.   OR   She, <u>consequently,</u> missed class.   OR   She missed class, <u>consequently</u>.   **4.** She was ill<u>, so</u> she missed class.   **5.** <u>Due to the fact that</u> she was ill, she missed class.   OR   She missed class <u>due to the fact that</u> she was ill.   **6.** She was ill. <u>Therefore,</u> she missed class.   OR   She, <u>therefore,</u> missed class.   OR   She missed class<u>, therefore</u>.

EXERCISE 8, p. 390. *Showing cause and effect.*

2. Emily has never wanted to return to the Yukon to live <u>because of</u> the severe winters.   OR   <u>Because of</u> the severe winters, Emily has never wanted to return to the Yukon to live.   **3.** It is important to wear a hat on cold days <u>since</u> we lose sixty percent of our body heat through our head.   OR   <u>Since</u> we lose sixty percent of our body heat through our head, it is important to wear a hat on cold days.   **4.** When I was in my teens and twenties, it was easy for me to get into an argument with my father, <u>for</u> both of us can be stubborn and opinionated.   **5.** <u>Due to the fact that</u> a camel can go completely without water for eight to ten days, it is an ideal animal for desert areas.   OR   A camel is an ideal animal for desert areas <u>due to the fact that</u> it can go completely without water for eight to ten days.   **6.** Bill's car wouldn't start. Therefore, he couldn't pick us up after the concert.   OR   He, <u>therefore,</u> couldn't pick us up after the concert.   OR   He couldn't pick us up after the concert, <u>therefore</u>. **7.** Robert did not pay close attention to what the travel agent said when he went to see her at her office last week, <u>so</u> he had to ask many of the same questions again the next time he talked to her.   **8.** A tomato is classified as a fruit, but most people consider it a vegetable <u>since</u> it is often eaten in salads along with lettuce, onions, cucumbers, and other vegetables.   OR   Since it is often eaten in salads along with lettuce, onions, cucumbers, and other vegetables, a tomato is classified as a fruit. **9.** <u>Due to</u> consumer demand for ivory, many African elephants are being slaughtered ruthlessly. <u>Consequently,</u> many people who care about saving these animals from extinction refuse to buy any item made from ivory.   OR   Many people who care about saving these animals from extinction, consequently, refuse to buy any item made from ivory.   OR   Many people who care about saving these animals from extinction refuse to buy any item made from ivory, <u>consequently</u>.   **10.** <u>Because</u> most 15th-century Europeans believed the world was flat and that a ship could conceivably sail off the end of the earth, many sailors of the time refused to venture forth with explorers into unknown waters.   OR   Many sailors of the 15th century refused to venture forth with explorers into unknown waters <u>because</u> most Europeans of the time believed the world was flat and that a ship could conceivably sail off the end of the earth.

EXERCISE 9, p. 391. *Using* SUCH . . . THAT *and* SO . . . THAT.

3. It was <u>such</u> an expensive car <u>that</u> we couldn't afford to buy it.   **4.** The car was <u>so</u> expensive <u>that</u> we couldn't afford to buy it.   **5.** The weather was <u>so</u> hot <u>that</u> you could fry an egg on the sidewalk.   **6.** During the summer, we had <u>such</u> hot and humid weather <u>that</u> it was uncomfortable just sitting in a chair doing nothing.
7. We're having <u>such</u> beautiful weather <u>that</u> I don't feel like going to work.   **8.** Ivan takes everything in life <u>so</u> seriously <u>that</u> he is unable to experience the small joys and pleasures of daily living.   **9.** I've met <u>so</u> many people in the last few days <u>that</u> I can't possibly remember all of their names.   **10.** Tommy ate <u>so</u> much candy <u>that</u> he got a stomachache.   **11.** There was <u>so</u> little traffic <u>that</u> it took us only ten minutes to get there.   **12.** In some countries, <u>so</u> few students are accepted by the universities <u>that</u> admission is virtually a guarantee of a good job upon graduation.

EXERCISE 10, p. 392. *Using* SUCH . . . THAT *and* SO . . . THAT.

2. Karen is <u>such</u> a good pianist <u>that</u> I'm surprised she didn't go into music professionally.   **3.** The radio was <u>so</u> loud <u>that</u> I couldn't hear what Michael was saying.   **4.** Small animals in the forest move about <u>so</u> quickly <u>that</u> one can barely catch a glimpse of them.   **5.** Olga did <u>such</u> poor work <u>that</u> she was fired from her job.   **6.** The food was <u>so</u> hot <u>that</u> it burned my tongue.   **7.** There are <u>so</u> many leaves on a single tree <u>that</u> it is impossible to count them.   **8.** The tornado struck with <u>such</u> great force <u>that</u> it lifted automobiles off the ground.   **9.** Grandpa held me <u>so</u> tightly when he hugged me <u>that</u> I couldn't breathe for a moment.   **10.** <u>So</u> few students showed up for class <u>that</u> the teacher postponed the test.   **11.** Sally used <u>so</u> much paper when she was writing her report <u>that</u> the wastepaper basket overflowed.

EXERCISE 13, p. 393. *Using* SO . . . THAT.

5. Please be quiet <u>so (that)</u> I can hear what Sharon is saying.   **6.** I asked the children to be quiet <u>so (that)</u> I could hear what Sharon was saying.   **7.** I'm going to cash a check <u>so (that)</u> I have / will have enough money to go to the market.
8. I cashed a check yesterday <u>so (that)</u> I would have enough money to go to the market.   **9.** Tonight Ann and Larry are going to hire a babysitter for their six-year-old child <u>so (that)</u> they can go out with some friends.   **10.** Last week, Ann and Larry hired a babysitter <u>so (that)</u> they could go to a dinner party at the home of Larry's boss.   **11.** Be sure to put the meat in the oven at 5:00 <u>so (that)</u> it will be/is ready to eat by 6:30.   **12.** Yesterday, I put the meat in the oven at 5:00 <u>so</u>

(that) it would be ready to eat by 6:30.   **13.** I'm going to leave the party early <u>so (that)</u> I will be able to get a good night's sleep tonight.   **14.** When it started to rain, Harry opened his umbrella <u>so (that)</u> he wouldn't get wet.   **15.** The little boy pretended to be sick <u>so (that)</u> he could stay home from school.   **16.** A lot of people were standing in front of me. I stood on tiptoes <u>so (that)</u> I could see the parade better.

EXERCISE 14, p. 394. *Using* SO . . . THAT.
   2. I turned on the radio <u>so that</u> I could listen to the news.   **3.** I need to buy some detergent <u>so that</u> I can wash my clothes.   **4.** Roberto fixed the leak in the boat <u>so that</u> it wouldn't sink.   **5.** Mr. Kwan is studying the history and government of Canada <u>so that</u> he can become a Canadian citizen.   **6.** Mrs. Gow put on her reading glasses <u>so that</u> she could read the fine print at the bottom of the contract.   **7.** Jane is taking a course in auto mechanics <u>so that</u> she can fix her own car.   **8.** Omar is working hard to impress his supervisor <u>so that</u> he will be considered for a promotion at his company.   **9.** Po is saving his money <u>so that</u> he can travel in Europe next summer.   **10.** During the parade, Toshi lifted his daughter to his shoulder <u>so that</u> she could see the dancers in the street.

EXERCISE 15, p. 394. *Using* SO . . . THAT.
   Possible completions: **1.** I can make out this check.   **2.** He needs to study diligently   **3.** I wouldn't miss the news.   **4.** he wouldn't be hit by the speeding bus.   **5.** Samir set his alarm clock   **6.** I can see more of the countryside.   **7.** I went over to his house   **8.** Spiro works at two jobs   **9.** she can get a better job.   **10.** They prepared lots of delicious food   **11.** he could make a downpayment on a car.   **12.** Finish your chores early

EXERCISE 17, p. 395. *Showing contrast (unexpected result).*
   PART I.   **4.** but   **5.** Nevertheless   **6.** Even though   **7.** even though   **8.** but   **9.** Nevertheless

   PART II.   **10.** However   **11.** yet   **12.** Although   **13.** yet   **14.** Although   **15.** However

EXERCISE 18, p. 396. *Showing contrast (unexpected result).*
   2. Anna's father gave her some good advice, but she didn't follow it.   **3.** Even though Anna's father gave her some good advice, she didn't follow it.   **4.** Anna's father gave her some good advice. She did not follow it, however.   **5.** Thomas was thirsty. I offered him some water. He refused it.   **6.** *(no change)*

7. Thomas was thirsty. **Nevertheless,** he refused the glass of water I brought him.

8. Thomas was thirsty, yet he refused to drink the water that I offered him.

EXERCISE 20, p. 397. *Showing opposition (unexpected result).*

Possible completions: **1.** I had a cold, but I <u>stayed up late studying</u> anyway.
2. Even though I had a cold, I <u>felt I had to finish my work</u>. **3.** Although I didn't study, <u>I did well on the test</u>. **4.** I didn't study, but <u>I did well on the test</u> anyway.
5. I got an "A" on the test even though <u>I hadn't done any extra studying</u>. **6.** Even though Howard is a careful driver, <u>he had an accident</u>. **7.** Even though the food they served for dinner tasted terrible, <u>I finished my plate because I was hungry</u>.
8. My shirt still has coffee stains on it even though <u>I have washed it twice</u>.
9. I still trust him even though <u>he lied to me</u>. **10.** Even though he was drowning, <u>no one tried to save him</u>. **11.** Although I tried to be very careful, <u>I spilled the coffee because my cup was too full</u>. **12.** Even though Ruth is one of my best friends, <u>I didn't invite her to my sister's birthday party</u>. **13.** It's still hot in here <u>even though I opened a window</u>. **14.** Even though I had a big breakfast, <u>I was hungry by 11:00 A.M.</u>

EXERCISE 21, p. 398. *Showing contrast (unexpected result).*

Sample sentences: **2.** I like living in a dorm in spite of / despite the noise.
OR I like living in a dorm despite / in spite of the fact that it is noisy. **3.** In spite of / Despite the hard work, they enjoyed themselves. OR In spite / Despite the fact that the work was hard, they enjoyed themselves. **4.** They wanted to climb the mountain in spite of / despite the danger. OR They wanted to climb the mountain in spite of / despite the fact that it was dangerous. **5.** In spite of / Despite the extremely hot weather, they went jogging in the park. OR In spite of / Despite the fact that the weather was extremely hot, they went jogging in the park. **6.** He is unhappy in spite of / despite his vast fortune. OR He is unhappy in spite of / despite the fact that he has a vast fortune.

EXERCISE 22, p. 398. *Showing contrast (unexpected result).*

Possible completions: **1.** I didn't particularly want to see that play, but I went anyway. **2.** He is very old, yet he still plays tennis at 6 o'clock every morning.
3. The plane took off 20 minutes late. **Nevertheless,** we arrived on schedule.
4. Even though she wanted a new bike for her birthday, the little girl was happy to get a new doll. **5.** I wanted to go somewhere exotic for my vacation. **However,** I had to go back home because it was my mother's 60th birthday. **6.** The teacher dismissed the class when they had completed the test even though the hour wasn't over. **7.** Although my daughter is only three years old, she knows all the words to

the "Alphabet Song."   **8.** She never went to school. **However,** she has done very well in her job despite her lack of education.   **9.** Despite the fact that my sister was visiting, I went to bed early.   **10.** I have decided to go to Thailand even though I can't speak a word of Thai.

EXERCISE 23, p. 399. *Showing direct contrast.*
1. Florida has a warm climate; *however,* Alaska has a cold climate.   OR   Florida has a warm climate. Alaska, *on the other hand,* has a cold climate.   **2.** Fred is a good student; *however,* his brother is lazy.   OR   Fred is a good student. His brother, *on the other hand,* is lazy.   **3.** In the United States, gambling casinos are not legal in most places; *however,* in my country it is possible to gamble in any city or town. OR   In the United States, gambling casinos are not legal in most places. In my country, *on the other hand,* it is possible to gamble in any city or town.   **4.** Sue and Ron are expecting a child. Sue is hoping for a boy; *however,* Ron is hoping for a girl.   OR   Sue is hoping for a boy. Ron, *on the other hand,* is hoping for a girl.   **5.** Old people in my country usually live with their children; *however,* the old in the United States often live by themselves.   OR   The old in the United States, *on the other hand,* often live by themselves.

EXERCISE 24, p. 399. *Showing direct contrast.*
2. the United Kingdom drive on the left-hand side.   **3.** sister's apartment is always neat.   **4.** makes friends easily and is very popular.   **5.** know about only house pets.   **6.** is easy to cut and shape.   **7.** is very outgoing.   **8.** some people are ambidextrous, which means that they can use either hand equally well.

EXERCISE 26, p. 400. *Showing cause and effect and contrast.*
2. because   **3.** despite the fact that / even though / although   **4.** because of   **5.** now that   **6.** , however,   **7.** . However,   OR   , but   **8.** . Therefore,   **9.** , however,   **10.** , but   **11.** although / even though / despite the fact that

EXERCISE 27, p. 401. *Using* OTHERWISE *and* OR (ELSE).
Possible sentences: **2.** You should / had better / have to / must leave now. Otherwise, you'll be late for class.   **3.** You should / had better / have to / must go to bed. Otherwise, your cold will get worse.   **4.** You should / had better / have to / must have a ticket. Otherwise, you can't get into the theater.   **5.** You should / had better / have to / must have a passport. Otherwise, you can't enter that country.   **6.** Tom should / had better / has to / must get a job soon. Otherwise, his family

won't have enough money for food.   **7.** You should / had better / have to / must speak both Japanese and Chinese fluently. Otherwise, you will not be considered for that job.   **8.** Mary should / had better / has to / must get a scholarship. Otherwise, she cannot go to school.   **9.** I am going to / should / had better / have to / must wash my clothes tonight. Otherwise, I won't have any clean clothes to wear tomorrow.

EXERCISE 28, p. 402. *Expressing conditions.*

Possible completions: **1.** I am going to finish this report even if it takes me all night.   **2.** We have no choice. We have to go by train whether we want to or not. **3.** I will go to the concert with you only if you will come to the basketball game with me next week.   **4.** Eric is very inconsiderate. He plays his CD player even if his roommate is trying to sleep.   **5.** I can't hang this picture unless you tell me if it's level.   **6.** Tomorrow I'd better get to the store. Otherwise, we will run out of food.   **7.** You should take your umbrella in case it rains.   **8.** I will help you move your piano only if no one else is available.   **9.** I will be happy to attend your party unless you have also invited my ex-wife.   **10.** You must take all your final exams. Otherwise, you can't graduate.

EXERCISE 29, p. 402. *Summary of connectives.*

Possible completions: **2.** I failed the exam because I did not study. **3.** Although I studied, I did not pass the exam.   **4.** I did not study. Therefore, I failed the exam. **5.** I did not study. However, I passed the exam.   **6.** I studied. Nevertheless, I failed the exam. **7.** Even though I did not study, I (still) passed the exam.   **8.** I did not study, so I did not pass the exam.   **9.** Since I did not study, I did not pass the exam. **10.** If I study for the test, I should pass it.   **11.** Unless I study for the test, I am sure to fail it.   **12.** I must study. Otherwise, I will surely fail the exam. **13.** Even if I study, I may still fail.   **14.** I did not study. Consequently, I failed the exam.   **15.** I did not study. Nonetheless, I passed the exam.   **16.** I will probably fail the test whether I study or not.   **17.** I failed the exam, for I did not study. **18.** I have to study so that I won't fail the exam.   **19.** Only if I study will I pass the exam.   **20.** I studied hard, yet I still failed the exam.   **21.** You'd better study, or else you will fail the exam.

EXERCISE 30, p. 403. *Summary of connectives.*

Expected completions: **1.** Because I was not hungry this morning, I did not eat breakfast.   **2.** Because I ate breakfast this morning, I'm not hungry now. **3.** Because I was hungry this morning, I ate a large breakfast.   **4.** I did not eat breakfast this morning even though I was hungry.   **5.** Although I was hungry this morning, I didn't have time to eat breakfast.   **6.** I was hungry this morning.

Therefore, I ate breakfast.   7. I was hungry this morning. Nevertheless, I didn't eat breakfast.   8. I was so hungry this morning that I ate a large breakfast.   9. I was not hungry this morning, but I ate breakfast anyway.   10. I ate breakfast this morning even though I wasn't hungry.   11. Since I did not eat breakfast this morning, I am hungry now.   12. I ate breakfast this morning. Nonetheless, I am hungry.   13. I was not hungry, so I didn't eat breakfast.   14. Even though I did not eat breakfast this morning, I'm not hungry now.   15. I never eat breakfast unless I'm hungry.   16. I always eat breakfast whether or not I'm hungry.   17. I eat breakfast even if I'm not hungry.   18. Now that I have eaten breakfast, I'm not hungry.   19. I eat breakfast only if I'm hungry.   20. I ate breakfast this morning, yet I'm hungry now.   21. Even if I am hungry, I don't eat breakfast.   22. I was not hungry. However, I ate breakfast this morning.

EXERCISE 32, p. 404. *Summary of connectives.*

Possible completions: 1. While some people are optimists, others are pessimists.   2. Even though he drank a glass of water, he was still thirsty.   3. Even if she invites me to her party, I will not go.   4. I have never been to Hawaii. My parents, however, have visited there twice.   5. I couldn't open the car door, for my arms were full of packages.   6. I need to borrow some money so that I can pay my rent on time.   7. The airport was closed due to fog. Therefore, our plane's departure was postponed.   8. The landing field was fogged in. Therefore, the airport was closed.   9. As soon as the violinist played the last note at the concert, the audience burst into applause.   10. Since neither my roommate nor I know how to cook, we took our visiting parents out to dinner.   11. I am not a superstitious person. Nevertheless, I don't walk under ladders. A paint can might fall on my head.   12. The crops will fail unless we get some rain soon.   13. Just as I was getting ready to eat dinner last night, the phone rang.   14. We must work quickly. Otherwise, we won't finish before dark.   15. Some children are noisy and wild. My brother's children, on the other hand, are very quiet and obedient.   16. According to the newspaper, now that hurricane season has arrived, we can expect bad weather at any time.   17. Ever since I can remember, my niece Melissa has been called "Missie" by her family.   18. Although my grades were high, I didn't get the scholarship.   19. The United States has no national health care, whereas Great Britain has socialized medicine.   20. I was tired; however, I felt I had to stay awake because I was babysitting. OR I was tired. However, I felt I had to stay awake because I was babysitting.   21. You must pay an income tax whether or not you agree with how the government spends it.   22. I was listening hard. Nevertheless, I could not understand what the person who was speaking was saying because she was standing too far from the microphone.

EXERCISE 33, p. 405. *Error analysis: general review.*

1. Unless I study very hard, I will <u>not</u> pass all of my exams.   **2.** My shoes and pants got <u>muddy even</u> though I walked carefully through the wet streets.   **3.** My neighborhood is quiet and safe. **However,** I always lock my doors.   **4.** Although I usually don't like Mexican food, ~~but~~ I liked the food I had at the Mexican restaurant last night.   OR   ~~Although~~ I usually don't like Mexican food, but I liked the food I had at the Mexican restaurant last night.   **5.** Although my room in the dormitory is very small, ~~but~~ I like it **because** it is a place where I can be by myself and <u>study</u> in peace and quiet. OR   ~~Although~~ **M**y room in the dormitory is very small, but I like it **because** it is a place where I can be by myself and <u>study</u> in peace and quiet.   **6.** <u>Even though</u> I prefer to be a history teacher, I am studying in the Business School in order ~~for I can~~ <u>to</u> get a job in industry.   OR   Despite <u>my preference</u> to be a history teacher, I am studying in the Business School in order ~~for I can~~ <u>to</u> get a job in industry.   **7.** A little girl approached the cage. **However,** when the tiger <u>showed</u> its teeth and <u>growled,</u> she <u>ran</u> to her mother **because** she was frightened.   **8.** Many of the people working to save our environment think that they are fighting a losing battle **because** big <u>business and</u> the government have not joined together to eliminate pollution.   **9.** The weather was so cold that I <u>didn't</u> like to leave my apartment.   OR   The weather <u>is</u> so cold that I don't like to leave my apartment.   **10.** I have to study four hour**s** every day because ~~of~~ my courses are difficult / because of my <u>difficult</u> courses ~~are~~ / because <u>of the difficulty</u> of my courses.   **11.** On the third day of our voyage, we sailed across a rough sea before ~~to~~ <u>reaching</u> the shore.   **12.** I can't understand the lectures in my psychology class. **Therefore,** my roommate lets me borrow her notes.   **13.** According to this legend, a man went in search of a hidden village. **He** finally found it after <u>walking</u> two hundred miles.   **14.** <u>Because</u> my country ~~it~~ is located in a subtropical area, ~~so~~ the weather is hot.   OR   My country ~~it~~ is located in a subtropical area, so the weather is hot.
15. I will stay <u>in</u> the **U**nited **S**tate**s** for two more year**s** **because** I want to finish my degree before <u>going / I go</u> home.

EXERCISE 35, p. 407. *Review: punctuation and capitalization.*

2. Although a computer has tremendous power and speed, it cannot think for itself. **A** human operator is needed to give a computer instructions, for it cannot initially tell itself what to do.   **3.** Being a lawyer in private practice, I work hard, but I do not go into my office on either Saturday or Sunday. **If** clients insist upon seeing me on those days, they have to come to my home.   **4.** Whenever the weather is nice, I walk to school, but when it is cold or wet, I either take the bus or get a ride with one of my friends. **Even** though my brother has a car, I never ask him to take me to school because he is very busy. **He** has a new job and has recently gotten married, so he doesn't have time to drive me to and from school anymore. **I** know he would give me a ride if I asked him to, but I don't want to bother him.   **5.** The common cold, which is the most

94

widespread of all diseases, continues to plague humanity despite the efforts of scientists to find its prevention and cure. **E**ven though colds are minor illnesses, they are one of the principal causes of absence from school and work. **P**eople of all ages get colds, but children and adults who live with children get them the most. **C**olds can be dangerous for elderly people because they can lead to other infections. **I** have had three colds so far this year. **I** eat the right kinds of food, get enough rest, and exercise regularly. **N**evertheless, I still get at least one cold a year.   **6.** Whenever my father goes fishing, we know we will have fish to eat for dinner, for even if he doesn't catch any, he stops at the fish market on his way home and buys some.

EXERCISE 36, p. 408. *Review: showing relationships.*
   2. If you really mean what you say, I'll give you one more chance, <u>but</u> you have to give me your best effort. <u>Otherwise</u>, you'll lose your job.   **3.** <u>Due to</u> the bad weather, I'm going to stay home. <u>Even if</u> the weather changes, I don't want to go to the picnic.   **4.** <u>Even though</u> the children had eaten lunch, they got hungry in the middle of the afternoon. <u>Therefore,</u> I took them to the market <u>so that</u> they could get some fruit for a snack <u>before</u> we went home for dinner.   **5.** <u>Whereas</u> Robert is totally exhausted after playing tennis, Marge isn't even tired <u>in spite of the fact</u> that she ran around a lot more during the game.   **6.** <u>While</u> many animals are most vulnerable to predators when they are grazing, giraffes are most vulnerable when they are drinking. They must spread their legs awkwardly in order to lower their long necks to the water in front of them. <u>Consequently,</u> it is difficult and time-consuming for them to stand up straight again to escape a predator. <u>However,</u> once they are up and running, they are faster than most of their predators.   **7.** <u>Even though</u> my boss promised me that I could have two full weeks, it seems that I can't take my vacation after all <u>because</u> I have to train the new personnel this summer. <u>If</u> I do not get a vacation in the fall either, I will be angry.
8. <u>Since</u> education, business, and government are all dependent on computers, it is advisable for all students to have basic computer skills <u>before</u> they graduate from high school and enter the work force or college. <u>Therefore,</u> a course called "Computer Literacy" has recently become a requirement for graduation from Westside High School. <u>If</u> you want more information about this course, you can call the academic counselor at the high school.

EXERCISE 37, p. 409. *Review: showing relationships.*
   Possible completions: **1.** I woke up this morning with a sore throat. Nevertheless, I went to work because I had to finish an important report.   **2.** I love cats. My sister, on the other hand, prefers dogs.   **3.** When a small, black insect landed on my arm, I screamed because it had startled me.   **4.** I don't eat desserts because I'm watching my weight. However, I had a piece of chocolate cake last night because it was my

sister's birthday.   **5.** Even though I told my supervisor I would finish the report by tomorrow, I really need another day to do a good job.   **6.** According to the newspaper, now that the speed limit has been raised, there will be more traffic accidents. Therefore, people will have to drive more carefully than ever before.   **7.** Since neither the man who gave me the information nor the manager was in, I said I would call back another time.   **8.** When people who are critical find fault with others, they should try to be more patient because no one is perfect.   **9.** Since I didn't know whose sweater I had found, I took it to the "Lost and Found" department.   **10.** Even though the library book which I was reading was overdue, I kept it until I had finished reading it.   **11.** What did the woman who came to the door say when you told her you weren't interested in her political views?   **12.** If what he said is true, we can expect more rain soon.   **13.** Because the man who donated his art collection to the museum wishes to remain anonymous, his name will not be mentioned in the museum guide.   **14.** Even though she didn't understand what the man who stopped her on the street wanted, she tried to be helpful.   **15.** Now that all of the students who plan to take the trip have signed up, we can reserve the hotel rooms.   **16.** Since the restaurant where we first met has burned down, we will have to celebrate our anniversary somewhere else.

EXERCISE 38, p. 410. *Error analysis: general review.*

1. We went shopping after <u>we</u> ate / after eating dinner**,** **b**ut the stores were closed. We had to go back home even <u>though</u> we hadn't found what <u>we were</u> looking for.   **2.** I want <u>to</u> explain that I know <u>a lot</u> of gramm**a**r, but <u>my problem is that I don't know</u> enough <u>vocabulary</u>.   **3.** When I got lost in the bus station**,** a kind man helped me**. H**e explained how to read the huge bus schedule on the wall, took me to the window to buy a ticket, and showed me where my bus was**. I** will always appreciate his kindness.

4. I had never <u>understood</u> the <u>importance</u> of <u>knowing</u> English ~~language~~ **u**ntil I worked at a large**,** international company.   **5.** <u>When</u> I was young**,** my father found an American woman to teach <u>my brothers and me</u> English, but when we <u>moved</u> to <u>another</u> town, my father wasn't able to find <u>another</u> teacher for <u>another</u> five years.   **6.** I was surprised to see the room that I was given at the dormitory **b**ecause there <u>wasn't</u> any furniture and <u>it was</u> dirty.   **7.** When I <u>met</u> Mr. Lee for the first time, we played ping pong at the student center**. E**ven though we <u>couldn't</u> communicate very well, ~~but~~ we had a good time.

8. Because the United States is a large ~~and also big~~ country, ~~it means that they're various kinds of people live there and~~ it has a diverse population.   **9.** My grammar class ~~was~~ <u>started</u> at 10:35. When the teacher came to class, she returned the last quiz to my classmates and me. After <u>that</u>, we ~~have~~ had another quiz.   **10.** If a wife has ~~a~~ <u>to</u> work, her husband should share the <u>housework</u> with her. If both of them help, the <u>housework</u> can be <u>finished</u> much faster.   **11.** The first time I went skiing**,** I was afraid to go down the hill, **b**ut somewhere ~~from~~ a little ~~corner of~~ voice in my head kept

96

shouting, "Why not! Give it a try. You'll make it!" After <u>standing</u> around for ten minutes without moving, <u>I finally decided</u> to go down that hill.

12. *Possible revision:* This is a story about a man <u>who</u> had a big garden. One day he was sleeping in his garden. <u>When</u> he woke up, **h**e ate some fruit, ~~Then he~~ picked some apples, and ~~he~~ walked to a small river ~~and~~ <u>where</u> he saw a beautiful woman ~~was~~ on the other side. ~~And~~ **H**e gave her some apples, and ~~then~~ she gave him a loaf of bread. The two of them walked back to the garden. ~~Then~~ **S**ome children came and ~~were~~ <u>played</u> games with him. Everyone was laughing and smiling, <u>but when</u> one child destroyed a flower, ~~and~~ the man became angry and ~~he~~ said to them, "Get out of here!" <u>So</u> the children ~~left~~ and the beautiful woman left. Then the man built a wall around his garden and would not let anyone in. He stayed in his garden all alone for the rest of his life.

~~~~~~~~~~~~~~~~~
~~~~~~~~~~~~~~~~~

Chapter Twenty: CONDITIONAL SENTENCES AND WISHES

EXERCISE 1, p. 412. *Preview: conditional sentences.*
   2. a. no b. yes c. no   **3.** a. yes b. no c. yes   **4.** a. no b. yes
   5. a. yes b. no   c. no   **6.** a. no   b. yes   **7.** a. yes   b. no
   8. a. no b. no c. yes

EXERCISE 2, p. 413. *Basic verb forms in conditional sentences.*
   2. have . . . will write   **3.** had . . . would write   **4.** had . . . would write
   5. had had . . . would have written

EXERCISE 4, p. 415. *Present or future conditional sentences.*
   2. would bake   **3.** have   **4.** had   **5.** is   **6.** were   **7.** would not be
   . . . were   **8.** floats / will float   **9.** were . . . would not exist   **10.** does not
   arrive   **11.** were . . . would not want   **12.** would human beings live . . . were
   13. disappears / will disappear   **14.** had . . . would have to . . . would not be

EXERCISE 6, p. 417. *Activity: present conditionals.*

If there were only one village on earth and it had exactly 100 people, 51 of them would be women and 49 of them would be men.

More than half of the people in the village (57 of them) would be from Asia, the Middle East, and the South Pacific. Twenty-one of them would be from Europe, 14 from the Western Hemisphere, and 8 from Africa.

Half the people in the village would suffer from malnutrition.

Thirty of the villagers would be illiterate. Of those 30, 18 would be women and 12 would be men.

Only one person in the village of 100 people would have a college education.

Six of the villagers would own half of the village's wealth. The other half of the wealth would be shared among the remaining 94 villagers.

Thirty-three of the people would be below 15 years of age, while 10 would be over 65.

EXERCISE 7, p. 418. *Conditional sentences.*

1. have   **2.** had   **3.** had had   **4.** will go   **5.** would go   **6.** would have gone   **7.** is   **8.** were . . . would visit   **9.** had been . . . would have visited   **10.** had realized . . . would not have made   **11.** had read . . . would not have washed   **12.** B: would/could have come . . . washed . . . had told   A: would have come . . . had called

EXERCISE 8, p. 419. *Untrue in the past.*

1. But if I had known (that my friend was in the hospital), I would have visited her.
2. But if I had known (that you'd never met my friend), I would have introduced you.
3. But if I had known (that there was a meeting last night), I would have gone.
4. But if I had known (that my friend's parents were in town), I would have invited them to dinner.   **5.** But if I had known (that you wanted to go to the soccer game), I would have bought a ticket for you.   **6.** But if I had known (that you were at home last night), I would have visited you.   **7.** But if I had known (that my sister wanted a gold necklace for her birthday), I would have bought her one.   **8.** But if I had known (that you had a problem), I would have offered to help.

EXERCISE 9, p. 420. *Untrue conditionals.*

2. But if there were a screen on the window, there wouldn't be so many bugs in the room.   **3.** But if I had had enough money, I would have bought a bicycle.   **4.** But if I did have enough money, I would buy a bicycle.   **5.** But if you had listened to me, you wouldn't have gotten into so much trouble.   **6.** But if she had not received immediate medical attention, she would have died.   **7.** But if she had passed the entrance examination, she would have been admitted to the university.   **8.** But if we had stopped at the service station, we wouldn't have run out of gas.

EXERCISE 10, p. 420. *Untrue conditional sentences.*
Possible completions: **1.** If I had been absent from class yesterday, I would have missed a quiz.   **2.** If I had enough energy today, I would move the living room furniture.   **3.** If ocean water weren't salty, we could drink it.   **4.** If our teacher didn't like his/her job, he/she would change professions.   **5.** If people had wings, we wouldn't have to rely on cars or other means of transportation.   **6.** If you had asked for my opinion, I would have given it to you.   **7.** If water weren't heavier than air, the earth as we know it couldn't exist.   **8.** If most nations didn't support world trade agreements, international trade would be impossible.

EXERCISE 11, p. 421. *Review: conditional sentences.*
1. were . . . would tell   **2.** had had . . . would have taken   **3.** have . . . will give   **4.** had . . . wouldn't have to   **5.** had been . . . wouldn't have bitten   **6.** would we use . . . didn't have   **7.** doesn't rain . . . will die . . . die . . . will go   **8.** had not collided . . . would not have become . . . would be . . . still existed . . . would be

EXERCISE 13, p. 422. *Conditional sentences.*
4. did   **5.** weren't   **6.** had   **7.** were   **8.** didn't   **9.** had   **10.** didn't   **11.** weren't   **12.** hadn't

EXERCISE 15, p. 423. *Using progressive verb forms in conditional sentences.*
2. But if she were here, the child wouldn't be crying.   **3.** But if you had been listening, you would have understood the directions.   **4.** But if he hadn't been driving too fast, he wouldn't have gotten a ticket.   **5.** But if I hadn't been listening to the radio, I wouldn't have heard the news bulletin.   **6.** But if it weren't broken, Grandpa would be wearing it.   **7.** But if you hadn't been sleeping, I would have told you the news as soon as I heard it.   **8.** But if I weren't enjoying myself, I would leave.

EXERCISE 16, p. 424. *Using "mixed time" in conditional sentences.*
2. But if you hadn't left the door open, the room wouldn't be full of flies.
3. But if you had gone to bed at a reasonable hour last night, you wouldn't be tired this morning.   **4.** But if I had finished my report yesterday, I could begin a new project today.   **5.** But if she had followed the doctor's orders, she wouldn't be sick

today.　　**6.** But if I were you, I would have told him the truth.　　**7.** But if I knew something about plumbing, I could/would fix the leak in the sink myself.　　**8.** But if I hadn't received a good job offer from the oil company, I would seriously consider taking the job with the electronics firm.

EXERCISE 17, p. 425. *Omitting* IF.

　　2. Were I you, I wouldn't do that.　　**3.** Had they realized the danger, they would have done it differently.　　**4.** Were I your teacher, I would insist you do better work.　　**5.** Should you change your mind, please let me know immediately.
6. She would have gotten the job had she been better prepared.　　**7.** Were I you, I would look for another job.　　**8.** Should you need to reach me, I'll be at the Hilton Hotel in Seoul.　　**9.** Had they not dared to be different, the history of civilization would have to be rewritten.　　**10.** Should there be a global nuclear war, life on earth as we know it would end forever.

EXERCISE 18, p. 425. *Implied conditions.*

　　3. I would have answered the phone *if I had heard it ring.*　　**4.** I couldn't have finished the work *if you hadn't helped.*　　**5.** I would have gone to Nepal last summer *if I had had enough money.*　　**6.** *If I had not stepped on the brakes,* I would have hit the child on the bicycle.　　**7.** *If Olga had not turned down the volume on the tape player,* the neighbors probably would have called to complain about the noise.
8. *If Tarek had not had to quit school and find a job,* he would have finished his education.

EXERCISE 20, p. 426. *Review: conditional sentences.*

　　1. would spend　　**2.** would have sent　　**3.** is completed　　**4.** weren't snowing　　**5.** would have gone　　**6.** would be　　**7.** were . . . would be
8. had not been sleeping　　**9.** would forget . . . were not　　**10.** did not outnumber . . . could not eat　　**11.** A: were not　　B: would be sleeping
12. were . . . would not be　　**13.** would not be . . . had　　**14.** would have been
15. would not ride　　**16.** would not have come . . . had known　　**17.** will tell

EXERCISE 21, p. 427. *Review: conditional sentences.*

Sample completions:　　**1.** If it hadn't rained yesterday, we would have had our barbecue outdoors.　　**2.** If it weren't raining, we would be going to the park today.　　**3.** You would have passed the test had you studied for it.　　**4.** Otherwise, we would have missed the turn.　　**5.** Without electricity, modern life would be very different.　　**6.** If you hadn't reminded me about the meeting tonight, I would have forgotten about it.　　**7.** Should you need any help, please ask me for assistance.
8. If I could choose any profession I wanted, I would be an archeologist.

9. If I were at home right now, I would be taking a nap. **10.** Without your help yesterday, I could not have finished painting the kitchen. **11.** Were I you, I would forget your quarrel with your neighbor. **12.** What would you do if you had a chance to go to the moon? **13.** If I had the chance to live my childhood over again, I would keep a diary. **14.** Had I known the test would be so easy, I would not have stayed up late studying for it. **15.** Can you imagine what life would be like if humans had not discovered fire?

EXERCISE 25, p. 430. *Using* AS IF / AS THOUGH.

2. as if/as though it were her native tongue. **3.** as if/as though you'd seen a ghost. **4.** as if/as though they were people. **5.** as if/as though he were a general in the army. **6.** as if/as though I had climbed Mt. Everest. **7.** as if/as though he doesn't have a brain in his head. **8.** as if/as though we had known each other all of our lives. **9.** as if/as though a giant bulldozer had driven down Main Street. **10.** as if/as though I had wings and could fly. **11.** as if/as though he would burst. **12.** would . . . would . . . would . . . would

EXERCISE 26, p. 432. *Verb forms following* WISH.

2. were shining **3.** had gone **4.** knew **5.** had told **6.** were wearing **7.** had **8.** had gone **9.** could **10.** would lend **11.** were coming **12.** weren't going to give **13.** could meet **14.** had come **15.** were lying

EXERCISE 28, p. 433. *Verb forms following* WISH.

6. had **7.** could **8.** did **9.** had **10.** could **11.** would **12.** were **13.** had **14.** did **15.** were

EXERCISE 29, p. 434. *Using* WOULD *to make wishes.*

1. Rita wishes it would stop raining. Yoko also wishes it would stop raining.
2. Anna wishes Yoko would come to the concert. Anna wishes Yoko would change her mind. **3.** Bob's mother wishes Bob would shave off his beard. Bob probably wishes his mother didn't try to tell him what to do. **4.** Helen wishes Judy would pick up after herself, wash her dirty dishes, pick up her clothes and other stuff, and make her bed. Judy probably wishes Helen didn't nag her to pick up after herself.

EXERCISE 30, p. 435. *Using* WISH.

1. were . . . were **2.** had come . . . had come . . . would have had **3.** weren't . . . were not . . . could/would go **4.** had paid **5.** had **6.** would turn **7.** A: were lying B: were **8.** A: didn't have B: were **9.** had **10.** had not gone **11.** would tell **12.** A: were wearing B: had known

Appendix: SUPPLEMENTARY GRAMMAR UNITS

EXERCISE 1, p. A2. *Subjects, verbs, and objects.*

              S   V   O   S   V   O

2. The <u>mechanic</u> <u>repaired</u> the <u>engine</u>.   3. Those <u>boxes</u> <u>contain</u> old <u>photographs</u>.

              S   V   O   S   V   O

4. The <u>teacher</u> <u>canceled</u> the <u>test</u>.   5. An <u>earthquake</u> <u>destroyed</u> the <u>village</u>.

             S   V   O

6. All <u>birds</u> <u>have</u> <u>feathers</u>.

List of nouns: politician, taxes, mechanic, engine, boxes, photographs, teacher, test, earthquake, village, birds, feathers

EXERCISE 2, p. A2. *Transitive vs. intransitive verbs.*

3. divided = VT   4. sneezed = VI   5. happened = VI   6. bought = VT

7. won = VT   8. won = VI   9. disappeared = VI — shone = VI   10. boiled = VT — made = VT — drank = VT

EXERCISE 3, p. A3. *Identifying prepositions.*

                                          P   O of P

2. The waiter cleared the dirty dishes <u>from our table</u>

                  P   O of P

3. I parked the car <u>in the garage</u>.

             P   O of P

4. Trees fell <u>during the violent storm</u>.

              P O of P   P   O of P

5. Cowboys depended <u>on horses</u>   <u>for transportation</u>.

             P O of P   P   O of P

6. We walked <u>to the park</u>   <u>after class</u>.

EXERCISE 4, p. A3. *Sentence elements.*

       S   VT   O   PP

3. <u>Sally</u> <u>wore</u> her blue <u>suit</u> <u>to the meeting</u>.

       S   VT   O

4. <u>Beethoven</u> <u>wrote</u> nine <u>symphonies</u>.

```
          S      VI      PP
```
5. Bells originated in Asia.
```
          S    VT        O      PP
```
6. Plants need a reliable supply of water.
```
       S    VT      O          PP            PP              PP
```
7. We enjoyed the view of snowy mountains from the window of our hotel room.
```
         S    VI         PP              PP            PP         S   VI
```
8. The child sat between her parents on the sandy beach. Above her, an eagle flew
```
       PP
```
across the cloudless sky.

EXERCISE 5, p. A5. *Nouns, verbs, adjectives, adverbs.*
```
       ADJ           ADV         ADJ
```
2. A small child cried noisily in the third row of the theater.
```
       ADJ              ADV
```
3. The eager player waited impatiently for the start of the game.
```
       ADV    ADJ
```
4. An unusually large crowd came to the concert.
```
          ADV   ADJ              ADJ            ADJ
```
5. Arthur carefully repaired the antique vase with special glue.
```
          ADV    ADJ                    ADJ           ADV
```
6. On especially busy days, the telephone in the main office rings constantly.

Nouns: fire, house, child, row, theater, player, start, game, crowd, concert,
Arthur, vase, glue, days, telephone, office.   *Total nouns = 16*

Verbs: spread, cried, waited, came, repaired, rings.   *Total verbs = 6*

EXERCISE 6, p. A5. *Adjectives and adverbs.*
1. careless . . . carelessly   2. easy . . . easily   3. softly . . . soft   4. quietly
5. well . . . good

EXERCISE 7, p. A5. *Midsentence adverbs.*
2. Ted often studies at the library in the evening.   3. Ann is often at the library
in the evening too.   4. Fred has already finished studying for tomorrow's test.
5. Jack is seldom at home.   6. Does he always stay there?   7. He often goes
into town to hang around with his buddies.   8. You should always tell the truth.

EXERCISE 8, p. A6. *Linking verbs.*

1. easy . . . easily   **2.** comfortable   **3.** carefully   **4.** sad
5. cheerfully . . . cheerful   **6.** carefully . . . good   **7.** quiet . . . quietly
8. dark

EXERCISE 9, p. A7. *Nouns, verbs, adjectives, adverbs, prepositions.*

2. Whales = *noun*
   mammals = *noun*
   breathe = *verb*
   air = *noun*
3. dive = *verb*
   deeply = *adverb*
   beneath = *preposition*
   surface = *noun*
   under = *preposition*
   water = *noun*
   for = *preposition*
4. migrations = *noun*
   among = *preposition*
   swim = *verb*
   from = *preposition*
   to = *preposition*
   icy = *adjective*

5. highly = *adverb*
   trainable = *adjective*
   intelligent = *adjective*
   sensitive = *adjective*
   refused = *verb*
   Finally = *adverb*
   immediately = *adverb*
   took = *verb*
   shared = *verb*
6. smell = *noun*
   poor = *adjective*
   eyesight = *noun*
   extremely = *adverb*
   wide = *adjective*
   range = *noun*
   of = *preposition*
   sounds = *noun*
   use = *verb*
   sound = *noun*

7. with = *preposition*
   clicks = *noun*
   whistles = *noun*
   songs = *noun*
   gather = *verb*
   around = *preposition*
   communicate = *verb*
   through = *preposition*

EXERCISE 10, p. A9. *Forms of yes/no and information questions.*

1. Does she stay there? Where does she stay?   **2.** Is she staying there? Where is she staying?   **3.** Will she stay there? Where will she stay?   **4.** Is she going to stay there? Where is she going to stay?   **5.** Did they stay there? Where did they stay?   **6.** Will they be staying there? Where will they be staying? **7.** Should they stay there? Where should they stay?   **8.** Has he stayed there? Where has he stayed?   **9.** Has he been staying there? Where has he been staying? **10.** Is John there? Where is John?   **11.** Will John be there? Where will John be?   **12.** Has John been there? Where has John been?   **13.** Will Judy have been there? Where will Judy have been?   **14.** Were Ann and Tom married there? Where were Ann and Tom married?   **15.** Should this package have been taken there? Where should this package have been taken?

EXERCISE 11, p. A11. *Information questions.*

1. Who is that letter from? **2.** Who wrote that letter? **3.** Whose coat is that? **4.** When are Alice and John going to get married? **5.** What color are her eyes? **6.** What color is her hair? **7.** What kind of tea would you like? OR What would you like? **8.** What do you usually drink with your breakfast? **9.** What made her sneeze? **10.** How long does it usually take you to eat breakfast? **11.** How did you get to the airport? **12.** What does the boy have in his pocket? [*also possible:* What has the boy in his pocket?] **13.** How many brothers and sisters do you have? **14.** Where did you grow up? **15.** How long does it take to get there by plane? **16.** What kind of novels do you like to read? OR What do you like to read? **17.** Which chapters will the test cover? OR What will the test cover? **18.** Why were you late? OR How come you were late? **19.** How long has she been sick? **20.** How many people are you going to invite to your party? **21.** Which camera should I buy? **22.** Who discovered radium? **23.** What are we doing? **24.** How's everything going?

EXERCISE 13, p. A12. *Shortened yes/no questions.*

2. <u>Are you</u> expecting someone? **3.** <u>Did you</u> stay up late last night? **4.** <u>Have you</u> ever been there before? **5.** <u>Are you</u> nervous? **6.** <u>Do you</u> want a cup of coffee? **7.** <u>Have you</u> heard any news about your scholarship? **8.** A: <u>Are you</u> hungry? B: Yeah. <u>Are</u> you?

EXERCISE 14, p. A14. *Negative questions.*

1. No. **2.** A: Aren't you hungry? B: Yes. **3.** A: Didn't you sleep well? B: No. **4.** A: Doesn't it rise in the east? B: Yes, Annie. **5.** A: Don't you recognize him? B: No. **6.** Didn't he say he would be here by 4:00? B: Yes. **7.** A: Aren't you having a good time? B: No. **8.** B: Isn't the Mississippi the longest? A: No.

EXERCISE 15, p. A15. *Tag questions.*

2. isn't she **3.** will they **4.** won't you **5.** are there **6.** isn't it **7.** isn't he **8.** hasn't he **9.** doesn't he [*also possible:* hasn't he] **10.** can they? **11.** won't she **12.** wouldn't she **13.** are they **14.** have you **15.** isn't there **16.** can't they **17.** did they **18.** did it **19.** aren't I **20.** isn't it

EXERCISE 17, p. A17. *Contractions.*

PART I. **1.** "friend's" **2.** "friends're" **3.** "Tom's" **4.** "students've" **5.** "Bob'd" **6.** "Bob'd" **7.** "Ron'll" **8.** "window's" **9.** "windows're"

10. "Jane's"   **11.** "boys've"   **12.** "Sally'd"   **13.** "Sally'd"

PART II.   **14.** "Who's"   **15.** "Who're"   **16.** "Who's"   **17.** "What've"
18. "What'd"   **19.** "What'd"   **20.** "What'd"   **21.** "Why'd"
22. "When'll"   **23.** "How long'll"   **24.** "Where'm"   **25.** "Where'd"

EXERCISE 18, p. A18. *Using* NOT *and* NO.
2. no . . . not . . . not   **3.** No   **4.** no   **5.** not . . . not   **6.** no   **7.** not
8. no   **9.** no . . . no   **10.** not   **11.** no   **12.** not

EXERCISE 19, p. A20. *Error analysis: double negatives.*
2. I didn't see <u>anybody</u> OR I <u>saw</u> nobody.   **3.** I can't <u>ever</u> understand
him. OR I <u>can</u> never understand him.   **4.** He ~~doesn't~~ <u>likes</u> neither coffee nor tea.
OR He doesn't like <u>either</u> coffee <u>or</u> tea.   **5.** I <u>did</u> nothing. OR I didn't do
<u>anything</u>.   **6.** I <u>can</u> hardly hear the radio. OR I can't ~~hardly~~ hear the radio.
7. We <u>could</u> see nothing but sand. OR We couldn't see <u>anything</u> but sand.
8. Methods of horse training <u>have</u> barely changed at all in the last eight
centuries. OR Methods of horse training haven't ~~barely~~ changed at all in the last
eight centuries.

EXERCISE 20, p. A20. *Negative words.*
2. Seldom do I sleep past seven o'clock.   **3.** Hardly ever do I agree with her.
4. Never will I forget the wonderful people I have met here.   **5.** Never have I
known Rosa to be dishonest.   **6.** Scarcely ever does the mail arrive before noon.

EXERCISE 21, p. A22. *Prepositions.*
2. to   **3.** for   **4.** from   **5.** for   **6.** (up)on   **7.** from   **8.** in/at
9. to   **10.** in [*also possible:* at]   **11.** of   **12.** from   **13.** for
14. about   **15.** of

EXERCISE 22, p. A22. *Prepositions.*
1. for   **2.** to   **3.** (up)on   **4.** from   **5.** of   **6.** of   **7.** about
8. with   **9.** (up)on   **10.** for   **11.** from   **12.** to   **13.** for
14. of   **15.** for

EXERCISE 23, p. A23. *Prepositions.*
1. with   **2.** of   **3.** to   **4.** of   **5.** at   **6.** from   **7.** with
8. in   **9.** at   **10.** from   **11.** for   **12.** of   **13.** at/with
14. with   **15.** to

EXERCISE 24, p. A23. *Prepositions.*

1. to . . . for **2.** from **3.** with **4.** to **5.** (up)on **6.** of **7.** (up)on **8.** for . . . to **9.** about [*also possible:* of] **10.** of [*also possible:* about] **11.** of **12.** to **13.** of **14.** with **15.** to

EXERCISE 26, p. A25. *Using* SUCH AS.

Possible completions: **2.** such as bread and butter. **3.** such as a Honda or Nissan. **4.** such as cancer and heart disease. **5.** such as Iran and Iraq **6.** as tennis and soccer. **7.** as the printing press and the computer chip . . . such as the atomic bomb and bacterial weapons **8.** such as when I'm sick or when I'm trying to solve a difficult problem. **9.** such as history and mathematics . . . such as languages and science are difficult. **10.** such as when I'm at a theater or when I'm talking on the phone **11.** such as three and eleven . . . such as six and ten **12.** such as German and French . . . such as Chinese and Arabic

EXERCISE 27, p. A26. *Connectives to continue the same idea.*

Possible combinations: **1.** Furthermore, it has interesting special features. **2.** In addition, you should read as many magazines in English as you have time for. Watching television can also be helpful. **3.** Moreover, a housing shortage has developed. In addition, there are so many automobiles . . . . **4.** Physical exercise is also essential. In addition, sleep and rest should not be neglected.

EXERCISE 28, p. A26. *General review of verb forms.*

1. had never spoken [*also possible:* never spoke] **2.** hadn't come **3.** be **4.** wouldn't have come **5.** was stamped **6.** will probably continue / is probably going to continue . . . lives **7.** will have been **8.** going **9.** Having heard **10.** sitting **11.** have been produced **12.** would give / was going to give **13.** have known . . . met . . . was working [*also possible:* worked] **14.** had been . . . would have met **15.** were made **16.** have been standing . . . are **17.** would change . . . (would) decide **18.** understood / could understand **19.** Being . . . was respected / is respected **20.** would not exist [*also possible:* could not exist]

EXERCISE 29, p. A27. *General review of verb forms.*

1. coming . . . has learned **2.** had already given **3.** apply / should apply **4.** would have been **5.** would be / was going to be **6.** Sitting . . . watching **7.** had been informed **8.** was completely destroyed . . . had gone **9.** embarrassing **10.** were **11.** invited **12.** puzzled . . . puzzling . . . give . . . figure **13.** has been **14.** working . . . can/will be solved **15.** call

EXERCISE 30, p. A28. *General review of verb forms.*

(1) finish / have finished taking   (2) will also finish / will also have finished . . . have ever had   (3) have learned   (4) had anticipated / anticipated . . . coming

(5) Living . . . going   (6) have given [*also possible:* has given]   (7) to encounter . . . (to) interact   (8) would like   (9) arrived . . . knew

(10) needed . . . (in order) to communicate   (11) couldn't find . . . would use/ used   (12) (in order) to communicate   (13) Knowing   (14) was

(15) to make   (16) became   (17) Hoping to improve   (18) (to) understand . . . appearing   (19) were saying / said   (20) bored

(21) think   (22) were experiencing / experienced   (23) was doing

(24) had wanted . . . living   (25) studying   (26) began . . . had

(27) Not knowing   (28) to expect   (29) excited . . . finding

(30) chose . . . introduced   (31) sitting . . . talking   (32) were

(33) spoke / had to speak   (34) wouldn't / couldn't / didn't understand . . . was saying   (35) was pleasantly surprised . . . responded   (36) took . . . building

(37) progressed . . . found   (38) asked . . . spoke   (39) were

(40) hesitated to ask   (41) even interrupted . . . had never been   (42) not to be surprised   (43) sharing   (44) learning   (45) was   (46) am

(47) hadn't come . . . wouldn't have been   (48) could have / would have

(49) knew   (50) had . . . to make   (51) would be